D0006126

Leaders:

Eat What

You Serve

Leaders:

Eat What

You Serve

by

Judson Cornwall

© Copyright 1988—Judson Cornwall, Th.D.

All rights reserved. This book is protected under the copyright laws of the United States of America. This book may not be copied or reprinted for commercial gain or profit. The use of short quotations or occasional page copying for personal or group study is permitted and encouraged. Permission will be granted upon request. Unless otherwise identified, Scripture quotations are from *The New King James Version of the Bible*, © 1982 by Thomas Nelson, Inc., Nashville, Tennessee. Used by permission.

Scripture texts identified NIV are from *The Holy Bible, New International Version*, copyright ©1978, New York International Bible Society. Used by permission.

Scripture quotations identified RSV are from *The Revised Standard Version of the Bible*, copyrighted © 1946, 1952, 1971, 1973. Used by permission.

Scripture quotations identified Williams are from *The New Testament: A Private Translation in the Language of the People* by Charles B. Williams, copyright © 1958, Chicago Moody Press. Used by permission.

Scripture quotations identified Phillips are from *The New Testament in Modern English* translated by J.B. Phillips, copyright © 1958, 1959, 1960, 1972, The Macmillan Company.

Scripture quotations identified KNOX are from *The New Testament in the Translation of Monsignor Ronald Knox*, copyright 1944, Sheed and Ward, Inc.

Take note that the name satan and related names are not capitalized. We choose not to acknowledge him, even to the point of violating grammatical rules.

Destiny Image Publishers
P.O. Box 351
Shippensburg, PA 17257

"We Publish the Prophets"

ISBN 0-914903-59-4
Library of Congress Catalog Number 88-71461

For Worldwide Distribution
Printed in the U.S.A.

First printing: 1988
Second printing: 1988
Third printing: 1994

Destiny Image books are available through these fine distributors outside the United States:

Christian Growth, Inc.
Jalan Kilang-Timor, Singapore 0315

Lifestream
Nottingham, England

Rhema Ministries Trading
Randburg, South Africa

Salvation Book Centre
Petaling, Jaya, Malaysia

Successful Christian Living
Capetown, Rep. of South Africa

Vision Resources
Ponsonby, Auckland, New Zealand

WA Buchanan Company
Geebung, Queensland, Australia

Word Alive
Niverville, Manitoba, Canada

Inside the U.S., call toll free to order:
1-800-722-6774

Also by Judson Cornwall:

Let Us Praise
Let Us Draw Near
Let Us Abide
Let Us Enjoy Forgiveness
Let Us Be Holy
Heaven
Please Accept Me
Profiles of a Leader
Unfeigned Faith
Let Us See Jesus
Let God Arise
Let Us Get Together
Let Us Worship
Elements of Worship
Incense and Insurrection
Meeting God
Worship as Jesus Taught It
The Secret of Personal Prayer
Worship as David Lived It

Dedication

To M. E. [Chuck] and Betty Call, long-time friends, faithful pastors of the flock of God, and ministers who live what they preach.

Contents

Preface

Ministers are my life. I was raised in parsonages that kept an open-door policy to visiting ministers, and, since my father held an administrative office in his denomination for some years, ministerial problems were often discussed in our home. Because of this even though I entered the ministry at a very young age I was neither starry eyed nor naive. I knew that there were problems and pitfalls ahead of me, and I was certainly not disappointed.

For over two decades I have been traveling throughout America and the world investing a large percentage of my time ministering to ministers in a great variety of settings — sometimes from a conference platform, other times across a restaurant table. I have lectured and listened to ministers, and I have also counselled and cried with them.

Few professions accommodate as wide a variety of persons as the ministry does, for God chooses men and women; the formally educated and the self-taught; old and young; large and small; rich and poor; and every type of personality that has yet been catalogued. In spite of these differences, each is a precious, chosen servant of God, and I have learned to love each one I have met.

In my intense involvement with ministers I have repeatedly heard three "in phrases": *burnout, dropout,* and *forced out.* The first phrase is spoken of as a present reality; the second one as a possible threat, and the third phrase is mouthed as a dreadful fear. So common are these expressions that I have come to expect to hear one or more of them in the first half hour of every pastor's conversation with me.

The major buzzword among ministers today is *burnout.* Pastors seem to be convinced that they are cruelly overworked; traveling ministers talk of travel fatigue; and even lay ministers are leaving the smaller churches where they have been actively involved in the ministry and are joining the largest church in the area so they can hide in the balcony and become inactive for a season. When challenged they all claim to be *burned out.*

Across America special clinics are now conducted for burned-out ministers, and some retreat centers now open their doors to these exhausted men and women of God. There are even special hot lines to give counsel to these ministers. I certainly commend all of these restorative efforts, for an experienced minister is far too valuable to lose without at least trying to salvage him or her. But all of these efforts are after-the-fact actions. Cures are great, but preventatives are far greater. Given a choice between a present vaccination to prevent a physical illness or a future surgery to correct the effects of that illness, we would certainly choose inoculation.

Why are ministers so convinced that they are burned-out? Most of them have total control over their time and much of their circumstances. Does God drive them to exhaustion? Jesus certainly did not overwork His disciples, nor do we ever hear the Apostles claiming burnout. I do not deny the reality of burnout, but I doubt the necessity of it.

In space-age terminology, "rocket burnout" signifies fuel exhaustion. Could this be what ministers mean by "burnout"? I have come to believe that what is being experienced is nothing more or less than giving out more than we are taking in. We cannot compare ourselves to the solid-fuel rocket that has but one supply of energy available, for He Who commissioned us into His ministry has made an inexhaustible supply of energy available to us, but we must constantly refuel to keep going much as an airplane must refill its tanks after every major flight.

We ministers get burned out because we run out of fuel, even though we consistently give that fuel to others. The owner of a gas station cannot run his car on the amount of fuel available to his pumps; it is the amount of fuel in the tank of his car that determines how long he can keep driving. The same principle applies to any minister. Perhaps if we were partakers of what we are preaching we wouldn't experience exhaustion to the burnout stage. Likely we need an infusion of Christ's life more than we need a vacation from His work.

The second common phrase in the vocabulary of ministers today is *dropout*. They talk, almost enviously, of others who have dropped out of the ministry, and, after speaking of some hard places they are walking through, they admit that they, too, are considering dropping out of the ministry. It is not a buzzword but it is almost a byword. If *burnout* speaks of exhaustion I believe that *dropout* speaks of indecision.

Who promised that the ministry would always be peaceful and pleasant? It certainly was not the Lord! Look at the examples of the prophets, and reread the pages of Church history. Faithful ministry put Jeremiah in a dungeon, Peter in jail, and countless martyrs to death. If, when we get to heaven, we talk this over with Moses and the Apostles they will tell us that ministry is not only hard work, it is usually unappreciated and often rejected.

Unless we are reaping the harvest of another there will be dusty plowing, costly planting, and continual watering before there is a harvest; the world, the flesh, and the devil will contest our every action. The ministry is not like instant potatoes; it builds from the seed to a harvest.

Do we dare threaten to quit the ministry because the going is tough or the battle seems costly? Aren't soldiers, even officers, considered expendable in battle? Jesus Himself said, " 'No one, having put his hand to the plow, and looking back, is fit for the kingdom of God' " (Luke 9:62). We've been called and equipped for a task. Changing our minds about our consecration when money is exhausted, acceptance is low, or the pressure is severe is being AWOL — absent without leave. Men are court-martialed for this in wartime.

We need to honestly examine our commission. If we are self-appointed we can spare ourselves much pain and confusion by getting out of the ministry immediately and by serving Christ in the marketplace. But if we are genuinely called by God into the ministry of preaching and serving, then we should never entertain thoughts of quitting. When the pressure is on we should stand, not stop!

Charles H. Spurgeon used to tell his ministerial students that if God had called them into the ministry they should never stoop to become prime minister or king of England. Ours is such a high calling that any change is automatically a step down. How, then, can an offer from the commercial world be a temptation? If we cannot fully submit our wills to God, what is our message to others?

The issue should never be whether to retire from the ministry; our efforts should be to refire ourselves in that ministry. God has made ample provision for us to be renewed through relationship with Him in prayer and time spent in the Word and worship. Just as eating and sleeping renew us physically, eating what we are serving to others and resting in the faithfulness of the Lord will renew us spiritually.

If ministers are not complaining of exhaustion or indecision, they often express their insecurity by discussing a fellow minister who was *forced out* of the ministry. Sometimes it was by the action of the local church board, other times by denominational action, and occasionally it was the result of moral failure in the pastor, but whatever the cause he was out of a job contrary to his will.

Some forms of church government foster this intense feeling of insecurity. The pastor can be voted out in a church business meeting, or he can be reappointed or dismissed by denominational action. Ministers often feel that they alone face such insecurity, but they should look at professional ball players being traded from club to club or dropped completely at the end of the season, or they need to remind themselves of the counsel and advice they gave to the members of their congregations who lost their long-term jobs in a corporate merger or bankruptcy action.

While preaching to others that God is the source of all their needs we ministers sometimes fall into the trap of thinking that the local church or the denomination is our source. Who called and commissioned us? If it was God, then He is responsible to sustain us. It does not appear that many of the Bible prophets were sustained and supported by the persons to whom they ministered, but their needs were met.

There is no basis for insecurity if we keep our eyes on Jesus and regularly feed on Him. People may reject our ministry, but they cannot revoke our calling, for it is God's calling.

Even the prospect of being forced out of the ministry because of venal behavior is unnecessary. The minister who has learned to feed regularly upon the Lord will have his ego needs met in his relationship with God, and the resultant righteousness and holiness that accrue from that personal walk with God will enable him to withstand the temptations of the flesh. Sin is not necessary in any believer — even ministers — but when we cut ourselves off from God's provision for our lives we tend to accept the substitutes the world has to offer, and these usually violate the will of God for our lives.

Moral failure in a minister whose ministry has become very visible makes good press. Even in a world as amoral as ours has become there is still a desire that those who minister the things of God be morally pure. The sinner wants the pastor to be a saint.

Impurity in a minister of the Gospel is seldom a disease. It is an effect, not a cause. Merely setting high standards for ministers will not be sufficient to prevent decadent behavior, for the problem is seldom one of mental weakness or spiritual rebellion. It usually is rooted in a violation of God and the Word of God. When God's will is supreme in a minister's life, immorality will not be viewed as an option.

Immorality in a minister is usually rooted in a wrong attitude towards himself or herself. Pride and a sense of deserving set the stage for failure. Playing God, or setting oneself before the people as king can give the minister a sense of being above the laws that govern others. What is needed is a good relationship with God and a growing and open relationship with one's life partner.

The minister who eats what he serves will probably not have to worry much about the burnout, dropout, forced-out syndromes that plagued the nonparticipating minister. Perhaps a brief reexamination of the roles God has called us to play will freshly inspire us to drop the double standard and motivate us to sit where our people sit and eat what we serve them.

Judson Cornwall
Phoenix, Arizona, 1988

Chapter 1

Leaders as Professionals

"The Son of man came not to be ministered unto, but to minister" (Matthew 20:28, KJV)

Ask the average person today what a minister is, and he'll probably say, "A preacher," or perhaps, "Someone who pastors a church." These are common — and accepted — concepts, but they are backward concepts nonetheless. It is not the office that produces the ministry; it is the ministry that sometimes brings a person into an office. A minister need not be someone who serves as a church officer, although all church officers should be ministers, for, while every pastor should be a minister, not every minister is a pastor. Essentially, a minister is a person who receives something from Christ and shares it with others. Through the years the Church has divided these persons into professionals and nonprofessionals, but perhaps the gulf has become too great, for the ministry the Lord has left for His Church is far too vast to be fulfilled by the professionals alone. Actually, these professionals have been placed in the Body of Christ to further equip all persons to function effectively in the ministry that Christ has committed to them.

At the close of a singing worship session in one church, the pastor said, "I want all the ministers present to remain standing to be recognized. The rest of you may be seated."

All but five persons sat down.

"Will all of you please stand again," the pastor requested. "Perhaps you misunderstood me. I want all the ministers present to remain standing so that I may recognize them. All other persons may be seated."

Again, all but five persons took their seats.

"Once more, will all of you please stand," the pastor repeated. "Now think for a moment," he said. What have you been doing for the past hour as we have stood and sung unto the Lord? Haven't we all been ministering unto the Lord? Therefore we are all ministers, and all should have remained standing.

"Now," he continued, "will all the ministers please be seated while the pastors present remain standing to be recognized."

Thus, he dramatically made his point that all worshippers are ministers, while some persons, by virtue of their offices, are pastors, evangelists, teachers, and so on.

Because the English language adapts itself to fit current thinking, the term *minister* has come to be viewed as synonymous with a church office. Some congregations even prefer to refer to their pastor as their "minister," and the dictionary defines the word *minister* as "clergyman," but this is not the primary meaning of the term in the Bible. The most frequently used Hebrew word for *minister* is *shararth*, which according to *Strong's Concordance* means "to attend as a menial or worshipper; to contribute to — to do service — to wait on." In the New Testament, the Greek word used is *diakonos*, which comes from the root *diako*, meaning "to run errands." Strong interpreted *diakonos* as "an attendant or a waiter," and he said it is used in the New Testament to signify "a deacon, minister, or servant." In his *Dictionary of the Bible*, William Smith, L.L.D., said, "A third term, *diakonos* (from which comes our word deacon), is the one usually employed in relation to the ministry of the gospel: its application is twofold, — in a general sense to indicate ministers of any order, whether superior or inferior, and in a special sense to indicate an order of inferior ministers."

Jesus espoused this concept when He said, " 'You know that those who are considered rulers over the Gentiles lord it over them, and their great ones exercise authority over them. Yet it shall not be so among you; but whoever desires to become great among you shall be your servant' " (Mark 10:42, 43). Since the Greek word Christ used is *diakonos*, the King James Version says, "... shall be your minister." Service, not authority, is the key to Bible ministry. It will be this Biblical concept rather than modern usage that is intended throughout this book.

Over the years, a great gulf has formed between the pulpit and the pew. In the minds of many, all ministry must come from the pulpit and all finance must come from the pews, but this division between clergy and laity is artificial. All believers have received ministry from the Spirit and are expected to minister that same grace to others. From among those who have disciplined themselves to search for fresh food and serve it to the spiritually hungry, God chooses some to fill the offices of the Church on earth. The office does not make a minister, nor should it hinder the flow of ministry. In the realm of ministry, there is equality; in the positioning of officers, there is difference.

In current language, we would probably speak of amateur ministers and professional ministers, for one definition for "professional" given in *Webster's Seventh New Collegiate Dictionary* is "participating for gain or livelihood in an activity or field of endeavor often engaged in by amateurs." The difference between an amateur golfer and a pro golfer is that one pays to play, while the other expects to get paid for playing. This is also the basic difference between "lay ministry" and "clergy ministry." This is not to ignore the extra education and training the professional has taken, for all who step from the rank of amateur to that of professional know that they must make greater dedication and preparation to succeed in their new role.

That the Church can exist and grow without professionals in the ministry has been proven repeatedly. The latest example is the Church in China. But throughout the world, over the hundreds of years since Christ instituted the local church, the spiritual development of a congregation has usually been dependent upon the professional pastor. Nothing written in this book is intended to cast aspersions upon the professional aspect of the ministry; quite the contrary, for much of the book will address itself to those who, as I, have dedicated their entire lives to full-time ministry. These professionals are God's gift to the Church "for the equipping of the saints for the work of ministry, for the edifying of the body of Christ, till we all come to the unity of the faith and the knowledge of the Son of God, to a perfect man, to the measure of the stature of the fullness of Christ" (Ephesians 4:12,13). We thank God for the "apostles ... prophets ... evangelists ... pastors and teachers" He has given to the Church (*see* Ephesians 4:11), and we rejoice in God's provision of bishops, elders, and deacons (see[7] 1 Timothy 3). They have never been more needed than right now, for the greatest spiritual weakness in today's Church is seen in its leadership.

As vital as professional ministers are, these officers

and their offices cannot do away with the tremendous need for spiritual ministry flowing from all believing Christians. Nonetheless, growing congregations tend to depend more and more on their enlarging staffs for the very service and ministry that individual members once supplied to each other, and some of our megachurches now have staffs larger than the membership of other churches. If this is supplementary, it is a blessing, but if it is substitutionary, it can be a curse, for when the congregation is reduced to dues-paying spectators, the vital thrust of the New Testament Church is destroyed.

A church of my observation had experienced consecutive years of progressive growth. As attendance increased, buildings were added and the ministerial staff was enlarged. It appeared that there would never be an end to financial increase, but then the bottom dropped out of oil prices and the area slipped rapidly into its own recession.

Every possible cost-cutting measure was implemented, including drastic staff reductions. The pastor expected severe negative responses from the congregation when services that they had taken for granted were no longer available. Instead, the people testified, "We are spoiled brats who have been waited on hand and foot by our paid staff. Now it's time for us to go to work."

To the amazement of the pastor, the people in the congregation began to form volunteer groups to accept responsibility for specific tasks one week per month. It proved to be infectious, and others volunteered their services. The church not only went on, but it strengthened its family relationships and drew new members into its ranks even though most of the professionals were gone. Getting the people involved in the work of the ministry proved to be a needed tonic for that congregation, for they had been overfed and underexercised for a long season.

That the apostle Paul was a professional in the ministry of the Gospel seems self-evident, for although he often worked as a tentmaker for his support, he was highly trained, and he gave himself full time to the work of the ministry. His approach to teaching and preaching was both scholarly and proficient, and the anointing level that accompanied him as he pioneered new churches is an unquestioned evidence of God's calling and placement of him into the apostolic office and ministry. Furthermore, his writings form the backbone of the New Testament. Paul was no amateur.

What is often overlooked in the life of Paul was his close relationship with and confidence in the many "amateurs" who associated with him in the exercise of both his office and his ministry. The book of Acts records that he was often accompanied on his missionary journeys by "the physician Luke," and Romans says that he greeted "Erastus, the treasurer of the city" and many lay persons who labored with him (*see* Romans 16). In his letter to the Corinthians, Paul commended the household of Stephanas, saying that "they have devoted themselves to the ministry of the saints ... submit to such, and to everyone who works and labors with us" (1 Corinthians 16:15, 16). He sent Tychicus, "a beloved brother and faithful minister in the Lord," to the Ephesians to "make all things known to you ... that you may know our affairs, and that he may comfort your hearts" (Ephesians 6:21, 22); he told the Church at Colossae, "Say to Archippus, 'Take heed to the ministry which you have received in the Lord, that you may fulfill it' " (Colossians 4:17). His special mention of Erastus, Tropohimus, Eubulus, Pudens, Linus, and Claudia (*see* 2 Timothy 4:20, 21); his instruction to Titus to "send Zenas the lawyer and Apollos on their journey with haste, that they may lack nothing" (Titus 3:13); and his intercession for the runaway slave, Onesimus (*see* Philemon); indicate the high esteem Paul had for these converts of his who had opened themselves to receive from the Lord and then were sharing with others what they received. No indication is given that any of these were "professionals," but each was a minister in the highest sense, and their names are lovingly recorded in the Holy Scriptures. It is unlikely that any of these persons held offices in the Church, but Christ's ministry flowed through them, bringing health and strength to local congregations.

Paul consistently spoke of ministry as providing a service or a substance to fellow Christians. To the Corinthians, he wrote, "You are manifestly an epistle of Christ, ministered by us" (2 Corinthians 3:3), and added that "[God] also made us sufficient as ministers of the new covenant" (2 Corinthians 3:6). Having spoken of being transformed into the image of God by beholding the Lord, Paul observed, "Since we have this ministry ..." and went on to say, "We have this treasure in earthen vessels, that the excellence of the power may be of God and not of us" (2 Corinthians 4:1, 7). Paul felt that what we receive from God is a ministry the moment we consent to share it with another. He did not connect ministry with position so much as with performance. He said, "We give no offense in anything, that our ministry may not be blamed. But in all things we commend ourselves as ministers of God" (2 Corinthians 6:3, 4). Paul was not dependent upon outside ordination. He had inside information, and the very sharing of this became his ministry.

Toward the end of his second letter to the Corinthian church, he wrote, "Now concerning the ministering to the saints, it is superfluous for me to write to you" (2 Corinthians 9:2), and devoted the rest of the chapter to receiving an offering for the saints in need. The sharing of spiritual revelation is ministry, and the sharing of finances is also ministry. The key seems to be that we have received from the Lord something which we are sharing with the saints. This is New Testament ministry whether it is done by the senior pastor with his doctorate degree or by a teenager in a Sunday school class.

Perhaps the twentieth-century Church could profit by dispensing with the terms *clergy* and *laity* and combining them into the term *clayity*, for we are all made of the same clay, and we are all commissioned by the same Lord: " 'Freely you have received, freely give' " (Matthew 10:8). The offices have not, cannot, and will not be equally divided. God chooses His own leadership, but the ministry has already been equally divided through the indwelling Spirit of God. All recipients of grace have a ministry of grace if they will share it. All who have received light have a ministry of light if they will shine it. Those who have met the Savior can introduce others to Him, and those who have found life in the Spirit can dispense this life to those who lack it.

The key to effective ministry is less mental preparation and more making the Gospel part of daily life, for ministers are only persons who have received from God a great gift that they desire to share with others. Unless we have received something, we have nothing to share with others. As David DuPlessis used to say, "If God pumps, I'll pour." We do not have that pump, but our life is a container that can receive and dispense. In that process we become partakers of the very ministry we submit to others. Furthermore, whether we are clergy or laity, we must first make spiritual principles work in our individual lives before trying to teach them to others, for if it won't work in us, it won't work in them, either. We have been called to share ministry, not theories. David's plea "Oh, taste and see that the LORD is good" (Psalm 34:8) needs to be heeded by all who yearn to be needed. We must eat what we serve!

Prayer:

Lord, I'll never understand why You chose me to minister on Your behalf, but I thank You that You did. Please help me to keep my eyes on You and to treat Your calling as a sacred trust. I make myself available to You for whatever task You may choose, and I do not care who gets the credit for what is done. In the midst of my ministry, may I never lose sight of my humanity and personhood, and please help me to accept myself as You have accepted me. Amen!

Chapter 2

Leaders as Persons

"Unless you eat the flesh of the Son of Man and drink His blood, you have no life in you" (John 6:53)

In America's religious system, we are so caught up in roles, offices, positions and titles that even the professional ministers often lose sight of their personhood. Much of the so-called "ministerial burnout" is little more than a loss of identity as a person while filling multiple roles. The Right Reverend Fillarole, Th.D., is a case in point. Pastor of the large First Downtown Church of the Observers, he supervises a large staff of workers, has a daily radio program, and appears on a weekly telecast in addition to handling multiple Sunday morning services, the Sunday evening service, and a midweek service. He counsels the distressed, supervises the budget, oversees all enlargement of the plant's facilities, and conducts the weddings and funerals of his parishioners. His is an ever changing role, and he is often caught with one hat in his hand and another on his head.

His dedication to the multiple tasks at hand have made him successful in the eyes of his congregation and his denomination, and he would be a formidable competitor in almost any business endeavor if he were in commerce instead of religion. Unfortunately, however, he has become more business than man. While he fills his roles most effectively, he consistently loses touch with his own person and therefore with the persons in his parish. In the eyes of the congregation, he sits on a pedestal like a hero, but he is as unapproachable to most of them as is the president of the United States. Even in his own home, he is more "lord and master" than husband and father. His roles have replaced his personhood, and religious authority has displaced spiritual ministry. While his congregation grows numerically, it groans spiritually.

The Need for Manhood in the Ministry

In order for man to relate to God, it became necessary for God to become man. God tried direct communication with men, but when He spoke to Israel from Sinai, it so terrorized the people that they pled with Him to never talk with them again. It seems that most denominations have done the same. When His voice was rejected, God appeared in theophanic form, usually as "the Angel of the Lord," and men expected to drop dead because they had seen an angel. Next, God spoke to men through the prophets; this so angered the recipients of the messages that they stoned the prophets to death, and their sons built tombs for the bones of the prophets.

It became obvious to God that man could respond only to his own kind, so "the Word became flesh and dwelt among us, and we beheld His glory, the glory as of the only begotten of the Father, full of grace and truth" (John 1:14). It was not when the Word was sent, but when the Word became what we are, that we were able to receive it. Sin so separated us from God that we could not respond high enough to touch God, so Christ, in Divine grace, descended to our level so we could relate intimately to Him.

Men need God, but they can be personally introduced to Him only through another person. The unconverted do not possess an intimate knowledge of God, even if they are active members of a church. Paul declared, "In the wisdom of God, the world through wisdom did not know God" (1 Corinthians 1:21), "And even as they did not like to retain God in their knowledge, God gave them over to a debased mind" (Romans 1:28). These may see evidences of God in nature, and they may have an inner instinctive awareness of a higher Being, but they do not know God.

God has purposed to reveal Himself through human flesh, not in nature. Jesus said, " 'Let your light so shine before men,that they may see your good works and glorify your Father in heaven' " (Matthew 5:16). So much of the time, we pray that God will do great works that will reveal the Father to our generation, but Jesus told us to do the great revealing works. Paul testified, "It pleased God, who separated me from my mother's womb and called me through His grace, to reveal His Son in me, that I might preach Him among the Gentiles" (Galatians 1:15, 16). He was separated and called in order for Christ to be revealed. Paul was necessary to the program of God, and so are we.

Yet ministers must maintain their manhood (or womanhood) to be of value to God. All attempts at being "Godlike" invalidate a person's usefulness, but even limited success in ministry tends to cause a person to play God. If we are fortunate enough to successfully counsel two persons in a row, we begin to think of ourselves as "God," but God has not called us as His replacement; we have been chosen to be His servant. We are invited to partake of God's nature, but God wants to share our humanity. When we play God, we separate ourselves from the very people God sent us to serve. We do not need an ornate pedestal on which to stand so others may look up to us; we need an exalted God Who is "high and lifted up" by a humble servant.

God wants to communicate to people through people. He needs a human personality through whom He can display His own Person. Jesus was so successful at this that His very enemies testified, " 'No man ever spoke like this Man!' " (John 7:46). The manhood of Christ was recognized, but the Divinity of God shone through. Similarly, on the day of Pentecost, "they ... began to speak with other tongues, as the Spirit gave them utterance"(Acts 2:4). The expression was human, but the inspiration was Divine. The humanity of the person involved was never dissolved by the coming of the Holy Spirit. The public praying of the preacher, "Lord, hide me behind the cross. May it be You, not me, Who is seen and heard" is at best wishful thinking, and at worst it is false pride rather than humility. The speaker *is* going to be seen and heard. What is desired is that the voice of the Father may come through the human instrumentality.

We should never despise our humanity; God loves it and needs it in His ministry among people. In filling the many roles that ministry may demand, we must be on guard lest we lose touch with our true selves. People do not relate well to offices; they relate to other people. The fear of allowing our humanity to show is unfounded, for congregations are not so bothered by our clay feet as they are disturbed by our shining halos.

The Need for More than Manhood in the Ministry

It was the God-Man Who brought man and God together, and it still requires this marvelous blending of the Divine and the human to bring men to God. Our humanity at its highest level is barely a step above the sinner at his lowest level, and often the morality of Christians does not exceed the morality of good men in the world. Men must see more than high standards and great dedication. They must see God in us.

The heart of Pauline theology is that God has chosen to dwell in the lives of believers. God the Spirit lives within us. He does not come merely to visit; He comes to reside in believers. Paul testified, "The mystery which has been hidden from ages and from generations, but now has been revealed to His saints ... is Christ in you, the hope of glory" (Colossians 1:26, 27). Paul, a Hebrew of the strict Pharisaical sect, was amazed at the revelation that God actually indwelt Gentiles and that this indwelling was God's chosen method of revealing glory to mankind. It is not our doctrines, dramas, dances, or degrees that reveal God. Only people indwelt by God can reveal God. Christ in you — the person — is the hope of glory.

It was not until there was God in man that man could see God, and it is interesting that God's servant is called "man of God." Timothy was told, "But you, O man of God, flee these things and pursue righteousness" (1 Timothy 6:11). "Man of God" is not a title or an office; it is a description of a person. Men and women of God are individuals in whom God dwells. This does not come through educational degrees, charismatic personalities, or church offices. It comes by having two lives active in one body. It is the demonstration of being continually indwelt by the Spirit and learning to "walk in the Spirit," be "led by the Spirit," and "live in the Spirit" (Galatians 5:16, 18, 25).

Being a "man of God" is not merely the result of an experience; it is the manifestation of a life that is above and beyond our mere physical life. It is the manifestation of Jesus in our ministry, much like the manifestation of the Father in the ministry of Jesus. It is the evidence of the Divine in the human being. Of the

unlearned fishermen, the Sanhedrin testified that
"they had been with Jesus" (Acts 4:13). Something
from within Peter and John radiated godliness until
the rough exterior was ignored and the Divine life was
acknowledged.

During Jesus' days on earth, the outstanding difference between Him and the rulers of religion in Jerusalem was His Divine life. It was obvious in His
teaching, for, "They were astonished at His teaching,
for He taught them as one having authority, and not as
the scribes" (Mark 1:22). It was just as unmistakable in
His miracles, for Peter preached, " 'Jesus of Nazareth,
a Man attested by God to you by miracles, wonders, and
signs which God did through Him in your midst, as you
yourselves also know' " (Acts 2:22). This difference was
further exemplified in Christ's authority over demons,
sickness, nature, and men.

This was no mere man, however anointed; this was
God in man. He chose to have no titular authority. He
was not even a part of the religious system; He was very
much apart from it. All of His authority came from the
indwelling presence of the Father. So must ours. What
He was, we must be. What He did, we must do. What He
demonstrated, we must demonstrate, for Jesus said,
" 'Most assuredly, I say to you, he who believes in Me,
the works that I do he will do also; and greater works
than these he will do, because I go to My Father' "
(John 14:12). Jesus Christ did not call men to go through
the world and tell stories about Him. He ordained
persons to go to the multitudes and do what He did, say
what He said, and exercise His authority here on the
earth. We are not merely preachers of righteousness;
we are revealers of a righteous God living within us.

The Source of this Divine Life in Us

Jesus said, " 'And this is the will of Him who sent Me,
that everyone who sees the Son and believes in Him

may have everlasting life' " (John 6:40). The Greek word He used for *everlasting* is *aionio*, which means "eternal." In the NIV, RSV, and LB, this phrase is translated, "should have eternal life," for the emphasis is not on the duration, since perpetuity of existence comes at natural birth. Everyone has "everlasting" life. Some will spend it in God's presence, while others will spend it in hell, forever separated from God.

Jesus offered His listeners "eternal" life. Entrance into eternal life comes at the new birth when the life of Christ takes residence in the convert. This eternal life is the life of the Eternal God, for that is one of the titles the Scriptures give to God. " 'The eternal God is your refuge, and underneath are the everlasting arms,' " cried Moses in his final blessing of Israel (Deuteronomy 33:27). Paul proclaimed, "Now to the King eternal, immortal, invisible, to God who alone is wise, be honor and glory forever and ever. Amen" (1 Timothy 1:17), while John wrote, "And this is the testimony: that God has given us eternal life, and this life is in His Son" (1 John 5:11). John had begun his epistle by saying, "That which was from the beginning, which we have heard, which we have seen with our eyes, which we have looked upon, and our hands have handled, concerning the Word of life — the life was manifested, and we have seen, and bear witness, and declare to you that eternal life which was with the Father and was manifested to us" (1 John 1:1, 2). "Eternal life" flows from the Eternal God through the Eternal Son.

"Eternal life" is not an experience — it is an entirely new source of life. Our initial entrance into it is an experience, just as birth is for natural life, but it demands sustenance or it will be lost. Natural birth must be followed by continuing processes to maintain the life that was given, and so must the new birth. Far too many ministers treat their conversion exper-ience as they treat water baptism — a one-time act of obedience — but assuming that one act of repentance will assure eternal life from that point on is a dangerous deception. The spiritual impotency of many who minister is sufficient evidence of the fallacy of this concept.

Jesus taught that the life of the Eternal is maintained by daily partaking of His life. He made this emphasis strikingly clear in John, chapter 6: " 'I am the bread which came down from heaven' " (v. 41); " 'I am the bread of life' " (v. 48); " 'I am the living bread which came down from heaven. If anyone eats of this bread, he will live forever; and the bread that I shall give is My flesh, which I shall give for the life of the world' " (v. 51); " 'unless you eat the flesh of the Son of Man and drink His blood, you have no life in you' " (v. 53); " 'it is the Spirit who gives life; the flesh profits nothing. The words that I speak to you are spirit, and they are life' " (v. 63).

In this graphic discourse to the multitude who had eaten of the loaves and fish He had miraculously provided the day before, Jesus likened Himself to the manna God had provided for Israel in the wilderness. The manna had to be gathered daily, and it was eaten several times a day. Similarly, Jesus alone is our source of eternal life, and we must feast upon Him at least daily to have this life as an ongoing circumstance. " 'Whoever eats My flesh and drinks My blood has eternal life,' " Jesus said (John 6:54). I do not view this as transubstantiation, nor is this a doctrine with ordinances. It is life transfusion by the digestive process. Eat and live!

Feasting on the Lord gives us life — it makes us communicants of Him. Before the giving of the law, God invited Moses and the elders of Israel partway up Mount Sinai to eat and drink with Him. He provided both the substance and the fellowship. Before Gethsemane and Calvary, Jesus ate with His disciples and instituted the Lord's Supper, providing them the elements of His body and His blood. Similarly, sitting at the table with Jesus and feasting on Him enables Him to progressively impart his eternal life to us. This life is necessary in order to have fellowship with God, for there is no fellowship with a corpse.

It is in times of prayer that we feast on Jesus. Prayer should be viewed as mealtime, not as request time, for prayer is sharing Christ's life and fellowship. Prayer is entering into the life of the Eternal. It is to a minister what manna was to an Israelite. It is the daily replenishing of spiritual life forces. It is the early-morning time of leaving the tent to see if God has once again provided daily sustenance for us. It is the exercise of faith that expects God's provision of life regardless of our activities the preceding day. Prayer, like the manna, is a supernatural provision made usable by the exercise of faith through discipline. The people couldn't grow the manna, and God wouldn't gather it for them. Similarly, we cannot produce eternal life, and God won't bring it to us. We must come to Him on a daily basis to be renewed in His life.

Neglect of the Source Brings Death

Every time Israel loathed the manna and demanded another source of food, God sent destroying plagues among them. Equally, whenever we reject the manna of Christ by refusing to pray, we not only set ourselves up for malnutrition, but we open ourselves to Divine judgment. Still, many of today's ministers are willing to do anything that will substitute for prayer. We have become so success-oriented that we believe we can do "it" in ourselves. We think a doctoral degree is the answer, and we use all the organizational skills we can muster. We attend all the church-growth conferences and learn methods and formulas, but we will not systematically come into God's presence for a renewal of eternal life to minister to the hungry in our congregations.

Somehow, ministers will not accept as literal the words of Christ: " 'It is the Spirit who gives life; the flesh profits nothing' " (John 6:23). We are convinced that the flesh profits greatly, or else we would not be making such a great display of flesh in our ministry. We seem to have convinced ourselves that the Spirit is not the only source of life, but we will never convince God of this, for the words of Jesus are indelible: " 'Unless you eat the flesh of the Son of Man and drink His blood, you have no life in you' " (John 6:53).

We may have had an entrance into life at conversion, and we may have received a Divine call into ministry. Men may even have ordained us into a religious office, but only daily partakers of Christ have continuing life, and life is the main product of our ministry. The fundamental difference between a corpse and a person is life. Each is well dressed, and each "looks very natural," but only the living can function. Only the living can bring life to the dying. Only those who are spiritually alive can intervene in facing spiritual death in others.

To do what Jesus did, and even more, we must have a continuing inflow of His life. If we are going to speak as He spoke, we must share His life. To teach with the authority with which He taught, we must partake of His life. To perform the miracles He performed, we must flow in His life. Any hope of exercising His authority over demons, sickness, nature, and men must rest in a great inflow of His life on a daily basis. To be demonstrators of His life, we must be partakers of that life. Otherwise, we will be displaying a counterfeit, and that is the specialty of the devil.

To the religious leaders of His day, Jesus said, " 'You search the Scriptures, for in them you think you have eternal life; and these are they which testify of Me. But you are not willing to come to Me that you may have life' " (John 5:39, 40). This is still the message of Jesus wherever ministers of religion and the Word gather. Life is in Jesus — not in the Scriptures. We can preach the Word of God and die spiritually. Our doctrines can be correct, but the heart can stop beating. We can contend for the inerrancy of the Bible and for verbal, plenary inspiration, and still lack the life of the Eternal, for this life is in a Person — Jesus Christ. The record is: "He who has the Son has life; he who does not have the Son of God does not have life" (1 John 5:12).

It is just that elementary. It is that essential. It is that exclusive. Jesus Christ is God's *only* source of life for any minister and ministry whether that minister is considered a professional or a lay person. If we accept this monopoly we shall live. To reject it is to die.

Ministers are persons who need to be indwelt by the Third Person of the Trinity. Our calling is always higher than our capability, but through an intimate relationship with God, through the Holy Spirit, we have access to the unlimited abilities of God. As men and women of God, we must blend the human and the Divine lives and share both of them in our ministries. We must see ourselves as dispensers of the life of God. Our first priority must be to keep our dispensers full, for people need the life of God; not merely the life of the minister. We cannot handle this in our human energies. We must consistently be partakers of the life of Christ. Unless we eat what we serve, the people will insist that we serve what we eat!

Prayer:

Thank You, Lord, that although You have chosen to use my humanity, You have also chosen to share Your Divine life with me by giving me eternal life — Your life. Please help me, for everything in life calls me away from Your presence and power. Please come against every substitute for Your life that I have brought into my ministry and return me to the simple relationship I had with You when You called me into the ministry years ago. In Jesus' name, Amen!

Chapter 3

Leaders as Prophets

" 'For out of the abundance of the heart the mouth speaks' " (Matthew 12:34)

God's first provision for Divine guidance outside the family unit, where the head of the household functioned as the priest, was the office of the prophet. We are told that "Enoch ... prophesied" (Jude 14), and he was only the seventh generation from Adam, so quite obviously the prophetic word began early. In God's economy, when He can find a person who will listen, He often commissions that person to become His spokesperson. This ability to clearly hear the voice of God is the one common denominator in all of the Bible prophets. While they represented almost every walk of life, they all had hearing ears, understanding hearts, and submitted wills. They heard, they comprehended, and they communicated God's word to others at His command.

We commonly think of the Old Testament prophets as foretellers, but while they did occasionally predict coming events, their most common ministry was forth-telling — speaking forth what God had communicated within them. They spoke for God far more than they foretold the future. They were preachers of righteousness, proclaimers of the Divine holiness, and promulgators of man's disobedient nature and inherent sinfulness. They have been characterized as men with their heads in the clouds and their feet in the dust of the earth. They were the channel of communication from heaven to earth and from God to man. This should be equally true of Divine prophets in this twentieth century.

The Prophetic Call

The prophetic office comes to a person by Divine choice, not by personal desire, training, or ecclesiastical appointment. Although the Bible speaks of the "school of the prophets," there is less reason to believe that this was a place where men were trained to be prophets than that it was a school where the prophets taught the things they had learned about God and His Word to others. When God calls a person to be a communicator for Himself, He makes him a prophet, not a parrot. God more than speaks a word in the ear; He imparts truth in the inward parts. He makes His message become a part of His man, and then shares that man and the message with the people.

Prophets are Divinely selected, not humanly elected. John the Baptist was declared a prophet by angelic announcement even before his birth, and God told Jeremiah, " 'Before I formed you in the womb I knew you; before you were born I sanctified you; and I ordained you a prophet to the nations' " (Jeremiah 1:5). Ezekiel, although born a priest, could not function as a priest in Babylonian captivity, so God simply appeared to him in a vision of a thunderstorm and changed his calling from priest to prophet. Once again we see proof that God calls whom He wills to do what He wills as long as He wills. The testimony of Amos probably reflects the circumstances of many other prophets. He wrote, "I was no prophet, nor was I a son of a prophet, but I was a herdsman and a tender of sycamore fruit. Then the LORD took me as I followed the flock, and the LORD said to me, 'Go, prophesy to My people Israel' " (Amos 7:14, 15).

There is no stereotype among those God calls to speak for Him. Paul, the educated, and Peter, the "unlearned," were poles apart, but each had a specific commission to speak on God's behalf. Elijah, the prophet of power, and Hosea, the prophet of pathos, were as different as day and night, as were Deborah, a judge, and Elizabeth, a priest's wife; yet God spoke prophetically to and through them all. Even by hindsight, which is traditionally twenty-twenty, we cannot see a pattern in God's choices for the prophetic office. In His sovereignty, He "does whatever pleases him" (Ecclesiastes 8:3).

It does seem, however, that God's choice is often based on the acceptability of a person to the ones to whom God sends them. The prophetic ministry is not a vocation — it is a calling. What we speak and where we speak it are not our prerogatives. God is far more capable at making these choices than are we. Ezekiel the priest was probably more acceptable to the captives than a member of royalty might have been, and Isaiah — of royal lineage — met with the approval of kings better than Amos proved to do. Similarly, Paul was a near failure among the Jews, but a very successful Apostle to the Gentiles. It is extremely rare for a minister to be universally accepted. Happy (and rare) is the minister who has found a place of acceptance and is willing to remain there. Far too often, success in a small field of ministry creates lustings to move on to larger fields, but Whose fields are these? And Who is in charge of the laborers?

Prophetic Enablings

God's callings must always be followed by His enablings, and this is never more true than in the prophetic office. Even though God may sovereignly choose a person to function in a prophetic ministry, there are many adjustments that must be made in that person before the prophetic Word can flow without great restrictions. Perhaps the first such adjustment is in the thinking of the person. Isaiah was caught up into the throne room for an adjustment in his concepts of God, and Ezekiel was given a vision of God's glory and of the glorious attendants at God's throne.

God may use visions, words, actions, or inward impressions, but before we can speak on God's behalf we need an adjustment in at least three areas of our thought patterns. We need an enlargement of our concepts about God, for the God we apprehend is too small to do what He says He will do. Most of us need a bigger God and a smaller devil in our thinking. We also need some major adjustments in our concepts about ourselves. We often carry mental images of ourselves that were formed long before we were transformed at Calvary, and we declare our insufficiency as though it were up to us to fulfill God's declarations. Furthermore, we need God's help to change our thoughts about the people to whom we will minister; we need to see them as God sees them through His eyes of grace. These conceptual adjustments are vital, "for as he thinks in his heart, so is he" (Proverbs 23:7). Even our faith cannot rise above our concepts.

When God is allowed to adjust the thinking of a prophet, He moves on to do some major adjustments in his life. On occasion God uses the prophet's life as an integral part of the prophecy. Sometimes this is an attention-getter, other times it is a visual reminder of God's message, and it often makes the prophet stand out in a crowd, like a bandage on a preacher's finger on Sunday morning.

Isaiah's life was a visual demonstration. His marriage to a prophetess was a sign to Israel. The name of his firstborn was a prophetic judgment: "Maher-Shalal-Hash-Baz" or "speed to the spoil" (Isaiah 8:1, 3). At God's command, Isaiah walked naked and barefoot " 'for a sign and a wonder against Egypt and Ethiopia' " (Isaiah 20:2, 3). Similarly, Ezekiel's life was regularly a prophetic message. God smote him with dumbness, allowing him to speak only when there was a prophetic message to give. He was made to lie on his left side for 390 days for a sign against Israel, and on his right side for 40 days as a sign against Judah (*see* Ezekiel 4:4-8). Furthermore, upon the death of his wife, Ezekiel was not allowed to mourn or weep, as a foretaste of the coming captivity (*see* Ezekiel 24:16). God seeks more than a mere proclaimer in His prophets; He wants a person who is willing to demonstrate His message.

In this altering work, God included an adjustment of the prophets' relationships with Himself. Moses met God in the burning bush before he was called to a prophetic ministry, and, when face to face with God, Isaiah volunteered, " 'Here am I! Send me' " (Isaiah 6:8). Again and again, Ezekiel had confrontations with God, for the person God chooses as His messenger will have an intimacy of relationship with God that goes beyond the rapport others enjoy. If something breaks this relationship, the ministry ceases! Prophetic ministry does not flow out of memory circuits. When the minister no longer hears God, he dares not speak for God.

The Prophetic Ministry

The New Testament speaks of both the office of prophet and the gift of prophecy. This gift is one of the nine gifts in the Corinthian list and functions in the realm of exhortation, edification, and comfort (*see* 1 Corinthians 14:3). Basically, it stirs up, builds up, and cheers up. Paul said that when the spirit of prophecy is present, "you can all prophesy one by one, that all may learn and all may be encouraged" (1 Corinthians 14:31). As useful as this gift may be, it is not to be equated with the office of a prophet. Both Testaments place the office of a prophet in the positions of guidance and government, while the gift of prophecy functions through the very ones who are being guided and governed.

In the Old Testament, prophets were often called *oracles* — persons through whom a deity is believed to speak — and in the New Testament we read, "Let them speak as the oracles of God" (1 Peter 4:11). Even the messages of the prophets were called "oracles"; in speaking of the Jews, Paul wrote, "To them were committed the oracles of God" (Romans 3:2).

These prophets were also classified as *heralds* — announcers of events. Lacking modern means of communication, heralds ran through the land with news of important events or recent proclamations. Perhaps this is the basis of the Divine statement "Surely the Lord GOD does nothing, unless He reveals His secret to His servants the prophets" (Amos 3:7). Heralds were also announcers of important persons. The entrance of royalty was preceded by a herald's proclamation. When Haman was asked by king Ahasuerus what would be considered high honor from the king to a subject, Haman said that it would be to dress the subject in a king's robe, mount him on the king's horse, and precede him through the streets by a herald crying, " 'Thus shall it be done to the man the king delights to honor' " (*see* Esther 6:1-11). Ministers with a prophetic anointing are heralds of God's presence and events. We proclaim His presence to those who do not recognize Him, and we declare His message throughout the land "with shouts of Grace, grace to it!" (Zechariah 4:7).

The Bible prophets were great *intercessors* who often pled with God for extended mercy to the people. They found no delight in proclaiming the messages of judgment. While faithfully saying what God told them to say, they interceded with God to change His mind and extend grace. They often repented for the sins of the people to whom they had been sent. May God give us more men and women who proclaim judgment through tears — persons who plead with God for mercy and repent for others until they can lead them into personal repentance.

The Prophetic Danger

The most obvious danger for any prophet is rejection. Jesus told the Pharisees, " 'Therefore you are witnesses against yourselves that you are sons of those who murdered the prophets' " (Matthew 23:31). Jeremiah and his message were repeatedly rejected — even when the Israelites pled with him to seek God for a word for them. The life of Amos was threatened, and he was banished from Israel. History records that godly Isaiah was placed in a tree and sawn asunder. He who walks in the ministry of a prophet should be prepared for rejection. God said, " 'I raised up some of your sons as prophets, and some of your young men as Nazarites. Is it not so, O you children of Israel?' says the LORD. 'But you gave the Nazarites wine to drink, and commanded the prophets saying, "Do not prophesy!" ' " (Amos 2:11-12). God does not always tell people what they want to hear, and people tend to confuse the message with the messenger. Furthermore, it always seems safer to throw stones at the prophets than at God.

Another prophetic danger is the pressure to speak before seeing or hearing from God. "Thus says the

LORD of hosts: 'Do not listen to the words of the prophets who prophesy to you. They make you worthless; they speak a vision of their own heart, not from the mouth of the LORD' " (Jeremiah 23:16). It is easy to respond to a situation with what seems to be a fitting word, but unless it is the word of the Lord, it is not a prophetic utterance. This may not be bad unless we put God's name on our word. Most prophets would admit that when a person is expected to speak for God and has not heard from God, there is a temptation to fake it. Yet Old Testament prophets often made kings wait for days until they actually received a message from God. This, of course, means days of waiting before God, but this is the calling of a prophet: to hear from God and to speak forth the message.

Prophets must also guard against telling people what they want to hear. How easy it is to respond to the cry of the people more than to the voice of God. People love to "prime" a messenger from God, hoping that he will tell them what they want to hear. It is amazingly easy to read this in the human spirit and to think that it is the Spirit of God. Isaiah was told, "This is a rebellious people, lying children, children who will not hear the law of the LORD; who say to the seers, 'Do not see,' and to the prophets, 'Do not prophesy to us right things; speak to us smooth things, prophesy deceits' " (Isaiah 30:9, 10). Micah, after a season of exercising his prophetic calling, declared," 'If a man should walk in a false spirit and speak a lie, saying, "I will prophesy to you of wine and drink," even he would be the prattler of this people' "(Micah 2:11). Sadly, few people really want to hear from God; they merely want God's approval upon their plans.

Still another danger a prophet must avoid is allowing the heart to be filled with wrong things, for " 'Out of the abundance of the heart the mouth speaks' " (Matthew 12:34). Not only our depravity, but also our humanity can interfere with a clear message from God through our lips. David wisely prayed, "Let the words of my mouth and the meditation of my heart be acceptable in Your sight, O LORD, my strength and my redeemer" (Psalm 19:14). What is often said of the computer can apply to the minds of prophets: "Trash in is trash out."

The Prophetic Responsibility

American religion is embracing organizers, kingdom-builders, entertainers, storytellers, pretenders, and deceivers. But God is still calling oracles, intercessors, inspired speakers, seers, proclaimers, and heralds. The true prophet is rarely popular, but he is very profitable to the Body Christ and the Kingdom of God.

For all of the dangers, pitfalls, and rejections surrounding the prophetic ministry, nothing is more profitable to a congregation than to hear the word of the Lord given with authority and faith. But this word needs to come from a person whose life demonstrates the message. A message of self-sacrifice given by one living in luxury becomes a conundrum to the listener. So the prophet's life will probably be out of step with society, for how can he condemn that in which he is a participant? His faith will be revealed in his behavior far more than in the tenor of his voice.

The prophet is also responsible for the words of his mouth. While every minister needs to honestly believe in what he is doing, the prophet must be certain that what he says is correct and coming from God. Otherwise, how can he impart faith to the listeners? The words of Jesus apply to all believers, but they are especially applicable to those who minister in the role of a prophet; while washing the feet of the disciples, He said, "If you know these things, blessed are you if you do them" (John 13:17). Certainly the prophet should eat what he serves.

Prayer:

Dear Lord, the weight of being Your prophet rests heavily upon me. I sometimes hear indistinctly and see with a distorted vision, and yet I know that You are speaking and revealing to me Your will for the lives of others. Please adjust my life and cleanse my heart until my ears are open to Your voice and my eyes see clearly the vision You would display before me. Help my life to be consistent with my words. I want to eat the very food that You have given me to serve to others. Don't ever let me forsake this living word that You are giving through me. Hold me in an iron grip. Channel my life in such a way that what I do brings You as much glory as what I say. Use me as long as I can contribute faithfully to Your Body here on earth, and then take me off the scene, lest failure in my latter days invalidate the ministry You gave me in my youth. In Jesus' name, Amen!

Chapter 4

Leaders as Priests

"Like priest, like people" (Hosea 4:9,
Modern Language Version)

Prophets afford a dynamic presentation of the Word and will of God, and they are often very magnetic individuals, but the Body of Christ also needs the calmer and more consistent ministry of a priest. Moses and Aaron illustrate the fundamental difference between charismatic and positional leadership. Moses was the aggressive leader whose authority came not so much from the office he held as from his forceful personality. Aaron, while admired and loved by the people, derived his authority primarily from his office. While Moses needed no special garments or other external signs to single him out as a leader, Aaron was recognized by his "sacral vestments," which endowed him with "dignity and adornment" (Exodus 28:2). Moses was a commander; Aaron occupied a command position. Moses was the patriarch; Aaron was the priest. Neither replaced the other, for both were needed in the leadership of this vast multitude of people that came out of Egypt.

In His economy, God has set three offices through which He extends leadership to His people: prophet, priest, and king. And He implemented them in that order. In the Old Testament, these offices were separated as a form of checks and balances, but in the New Testament the offices of priest and king seem to intertwine, for Jesus was declared to be prophet, priest, and king, and the book of Revelation declares that Christ has made us "kings and priests to His God and Father" (Revelation 1:6). The prophets spoke on God's behalf; the priests ministered on behalf of the people; the king was expected to unify the people under God's covenant laws. These Old Testament offices are carried into the New Testament as ministries, and though the titles of priest and king are not listed in the fivefold ministries of Ephesians, these functions are there under the titles of apostle and pastor-teacher.

The Levels of the Priesthood

The top authority in the Mosaic priesthood was the high priest. Before the Law was given, Melchizedek functioned as a high priest, and chapter five of the book of Hebrews presents him as a type with Christ as the antitype. Most Bible commentators see Melchizedek as an early theophanic manifestation of God in the Old Testament, and the New Testament declares Christ to be our present high priest: "Therefore, holy brethren, partakers of the heavenly calling, consider the Apostle and High Priest of our confession, Christ Jesus" (Hebrews 3:1); "we have a great High Priest who has passed through the heavens, Jesus the Son of God ..." (Hebrews 4:14). After the Law was given and the priesthood was activated, Aaron was appointed as high priest for the people, and all succession to this office came from his progeny.

The high priest performed certain ministries which were exclusively his. He alone could make atonement for the other priests and for the people (*see* Leviticus 16), and only he could wear the breastplate with the *Urim* and *Thummim* by which the will of God was discerned. He was the sole individual permitted to enter the Holy of Holies, and even then could only enter once a year. The consecration of other persons to the priesthood was His exclusive responsibility.

As our representative in the heavens, Christ has perfectly fulfilled all of these functions. He is the High Priest, and we are not. Transference of this office came at the death of the high priest, and our High Priest lives forever. No man on earth will ever hold this office.

The second level in the priesthood was the Aaronic priesthood. Before the giving of the Law, the father of each household functioned as a priest for his family; after the provisions of the Law were implemented, the Aaronic priesthood was instituted as a replacement for the heads of individual households, since God had accepted the entire nation as His family. In doing so, God localized the place of sacrifice at the tabernacle and formalized the rites of worship in the provisions of the Law. The means of approach was now God's prescribed way, and the complexity of the sacrifices and ordinances called for a professional priesthood.

In the New Testament, pastors, or elders, fulfill this ministry. In the listing of the ministry gifts (*see* Ephesians 4:11), *pastor* and *teacher* are connected in the Greek, and that pastor-teacher is charged to "do the work of an evangelist" (2 Timothy 4:5). The application of all scriptural means to the lives of believers is in the hands of the pastor, just as it was once in the hands of the priests. The office of the priest has not been destroyed; it has merely been renamed. Protestants should not shy away from the priesthood of a pastor just because the Catholics call their spiritual leaders "priests," for so do the Lutherans and the Episcopalians. While pastors are not high priests, they are sons of the High Priest who have been consecrated to the office of the priesthood by their Father in heaven.

The third level of the Old Testament priesthood was the Levitical priesthood. Because Aaron's family was small, and because half of the priests were killed by Divine judgment the very first day the priesthood functioned, God gave the entire tribe of Levi to help Aaron and his sons in the performance of their ministry. Although there was a wide range of activity prescribed for them, their ministry was confined to the outer court. They were responsible for supplying the wood for the Brazen Altar, for disposing of the ashes, for flaying the sacrificial animals, and for performing other services as Aaron's sons specified. So vital was their support ministry that, after the capture of the Promised Land, they were called "the Levitical priests."

The Levites were the Old Testament types of which believers are the New Testament fulfillment. The testimony is, " '[You] have made us kings and priests to our God; and we shall reign on the earth' " (Revelation 5:10). Just as the Levitical priesthood supplemented rather than replaced the Aaronic priesthood, so the priesthood of the believers is not to replace the priestly ministry of pastors; it is to augment it. Neither can function well without the other. Aaron and his sons could not do everything that was needed to help this vast number of people worship God, and neither can a local pastor. Levitical ministry is desperately needed in every local congregation.

Requirements for the Priesthood

Applications were never taken for the priesthood. Priests had to be born to the office (*see* Exodus 29:9). Only the sons of Aaron could belong to the Aaronic priesthood, and men had to be of the lineage of Levi to be Levitical priests. It goes without saying that only those born to the family of God can be priests unto God.

From among this lineage, men were selected to serve, but availability was no guarantee of acceptability. Nadab and Abihu, sons of Aaron, were rejected by God the first day they served. How difficult it seems to be for Bible school graduates who have volunteered for ministry to accept that God may not choose them for priestly service, for God does not do His work through volunteers — He conscripts His workers from among the volunteers.

The Levites began to study for their duties when they were about twenty-five years old, and they were consecrated as priests at age thirty. At age fifty they ceased serving the people and ministered exclusively to their brethren.

On their thirtieth birthday they were brought before the high priest to be invested or ordained into the priesthood. It was a seven-day ritual (*see* Exodus 29:30) during which they were stripped and then washed with water (*see* Exodus 40:12). At that time, they were examined for any physical defects that would prevent them from serving acceptably in God's priesthood, for "the LORD spoke to Moses, saying, 'Speak to Aaron, saying: "No man of your descendants in succeeding generations, who has any defect, may approach to offer the bread of his God" ' " (Leviticus 21:16, 18). God then delineated twelve disqualifying physical defects that, in spiritual application, are still in effect.

Verse 18 says that "A man blind" was automatically disqualified from service. Priests without spiritual vision are useless; as Jesus said, " 'If the blind leads the blind, both will fall into a ditch' " (Matthew 15:14). "A man ... lame" was unacceptable to the priesthood, for if the priests cannot walk the route, how can they lead others in it? The priesthood was demonstrated far more than it was declared, and it still is. A man with "a marred face" was rejected, and priests who have distorted the image of God are still barred from service. Paul spoke of "Christ in you, the hope of glory" (Colossians 1:27); we are God's only hope of revealed glory on this earth, and if He cannot be seen in our countenance, where can He be revealed?

A fourth disqualifying physical defect was " ... any limb too long." When anything is out of proportion, it calls attention to itself. A priest with too much flesh is still not allowed to serve, for our service and our walk are supposed to call attention to God, not to self. Even a man "who has a broken foot" was refused ordination to the priesthood. This is not a birth defect; it is the result of an injury that did not heal properly. A defect in our walk makes us useless in Christ's service, and this is especially true if the defect is caused by a wound we will not allow to heal properly. Similarly, a man "who has a broken hand" would be unable to offer anything to God. When the worshipper presented his gift to the priest, expecting to have it in turn presented to God, the broken-handed priest would drop the gift. Strong hands are needed for priestly ministries.

Verse 20 adds five other physical defects that disqualified a priest from serving in his office. "A hunchback" was set aside; ability to bear burdens was and still is a requirement for service. No priest has the right to put all of the burdens upon the intercessors of the congregation. "A dwarf" was not chosen, for one who has not attained unto the stature of Christ is not put into the leadership of the priesthood. Maturity in Christ is more valuable than talent and ability, but, unfortunately, many persons today are chosen far more for their natural abilities than for their spiritual maturity. This might be satisfactory in other spheres of activity, but it will never work in the priesthood.

"A man who has a defect in his eye" is useless in the priesthood. The priest who "sees men like trees" (Mark 8:24) can be dangerous in leadership, for blurred vision is nearly as great a hazard as blindness. A priest who was discovered to have "eczema" was also refused. The King James translates this as "scurvy," which is a skin disorder that is the result of an improper diet; it was the scourge of early sailing vessels. Modern priests who will not feed upon Christ and the Word will be disqualified when the eczema shows up. Improper spiritual diet will produce "itch or skin trouble" (Modern Language Version). Even a man who had a "scab" was unacceptable to the service of his God, for it was evidence of an unhealed wound, and the person who ministers with unhealed wounds risks a reopening of the old wound. When we have come to inner purity the scabs will fall off, showing complete healing. Until then, we are set aside.

The last defect listed is that of being "a eunuch" — one who, through the actions of others, has been deprived of his ability to reproduce. Jesus told His disciples, " 'I chose you and appointed you that you should go and bear fruit, and that your fruit should remain' " (John 15:16). Reproduction is vital to spiritual growth, and the leader who cannot reproduce is replaced.

These defects did not affect the birthright of these men — as priests they were provided for — but the defects did nullify their service to God and to the people. Our salvation is never dependent upon our perfection, but our service demands abilities that can be seriously impaired by any one of these twelve flaws. Paul told Timothy, "All Scripture is given by inspiration of God ... that the man of God may be complete, thoroughly equipped for every good work" (2 Timothy 3:16, 17). We don't need to learn to live with a defect, for God has provided healing for everything that would disqualify us from service, but the healing must precede the ordination.

When the physical examination revealed none of these disabilities, the priest was clothed with the holy garments (*see* Exodus 40:13) and sprinkled with blood from the sin sacrifice. Then blood was placed on the tip of the right ear, on the right thumb, and on the right big toe (*see* Exodus 29:20), signifying the consecration of his hearing, ministering, and walking. Every modern priest needs a special consecration on his hearing, service, and walk, for he will be functioning on behalf of many who have not yet experienced the power of the blood of Jesus.

The application of the blood was followed by wave offerings, or the heave offering (*see* Exodus 29). Finally, they ate the flesh of the ram and the loaf of bread that had been offered in the wave offering (*see* Exodus 32). This is a picture of eating Christ, Who is both the Lamb of God and the Bread of God. At the end of this seven-day ritual the young priest was consecrated into full-time service and began to serve in the rotational course assigned to his family.

The Duties of the Priesthood

The duties of the priesthood were multitudinous, but six of their prime duties have beautiful spiritual applications to pastor-priests in the ministry today. The first such duty was to maintain the sacred fire on the Brazen Altar. God had said, " 'Command Aaron and his sons, saying, "... the fire on the altar shall be kept burning on it ... it shall not be put out ... a perpetual fire shall burn on the altar; it shall never go out" ' " (Leviticus 6, 9, 12, 13). When the Tabernacle was first completed and Moses inaugurated the services of the priesthood, God sent fire from heaven upon the first sacrifice laid upon the Brazen Altar. God demanded that this fire be perpetuated. God supplied it initially, but the priests were expected to maintain it. This required regular replenishing of the wood and the removal of the ashes, and when the camp moved to a new site, the priests had to carry some of the embers of this fire in a special censer.

Priests must maintain the fire of God burning in their own hearts and lives. How easily we lose our early burning love for God and our joy of serving Him. The fire of our initial call and ordination often gets smothered with people and their problems. Similarly, the fire of revival and renewal in the Church needs to be kept ablaze by the priests. How short-lived are most revivals; once the original wood supply is consumed, the flame goes out, leaving us with a cooling ash heap and warm memories, but no fire.

It is common to blame the sins of the saints for the loss of the flame of God, but it was the task of the priest to maintain that fire, and it remains the responsibility of the priesthood. If we get so busy with administration that we fail to add fuel to the flickering flame, God will hold us, not the people, responsible for the loss of the sacred flame. Fasting and praying to seek a new flame is probably in vain, for God made us stewards of an initial flame. If we ignore it, He is more likely to give the flame to another than to return it to us, just as in our Lord's parable when the buried talent was given to another.

A second duty of the priesthood was the offering of sacrifices, many of which were for the expiation of sin. The priest assisted in the confession, explained the sacrifice, and sprinkled the shed blood. While the death of Christ has canceled all further bloody sacrifices, the part the priest played in offering them still remains. New Testament priests must help the sinning person find full atonement in Christ Jesus, for few can find it alone. We need to bring people into an awareness of

Christ's forgiveness and their restoration into full fellowship with God.

Some of the sacrifices were for the exhibition of thanksgiving. The peace offerings and thanks offerings were visible evidences of the appreciation and gratitude of the offerer. Just as then, people need assistance in exhibiting their thanksgiving in a tangible and demonstrative way. The giving of thanks is never automatic, but it is always acceptable. Often people need little more than some assistance from their priest in knowing how to genuinely thank God for Himself and His goodness to them.

Other sacrifices were for the expression of faith, because the slain animal did not make atonement for the people; their faith in God's provision cleansed them. They looked forward to Calvary, while we look back to it, but it has always been Christ Jesus Who makes atonement for sin. People need the assistance of their priest to continually approach God in faith. Sometimes, at the point of their greatest need, their confidence in God is at its lowest ebb. Frequently a teaching priest can renew their faith and help them to lay hold of God's provisions in a fresh way.

A third ministry of the priests was blessing the people. "The LORD spoke to Moses, saying: 'Speak to Aaron and his sons, saying, "This is the way you shall bless the children of Israel. Say to them: 'The LORD bless you and keep you; the LORD make His face shine upon you, and be gracious to you; the LORD lift up His countenance upon you, and give you peace.' " So they shall put My name on the children of Israel, and I will bless them' " (Numbers 6:22-27). People don't need to be condemned; they need to be blessed. Priests should bless, not bilk, the people. While we habitually say, "The Lord bless you," God instructs His priests to do that blessing. Who can measure the power of a priest's blessing? We need to learn to bless God's people, for that puts God's name upon them.

A fourth ministry entrusted to the Aaronic priesthood was the maintaining of the ministry of the Holy Place. The priests kept the oil supply of the Lampstand high, and they trimmed the wicks of the lamps. Priests today need to maintain a good balance between the supply of the Holy Spirit (the oil) and the amount of their humanity (the wick) that is exposed. If the wick is submerged too low, the flame will go out, but if it is raised too high, it will produce smoke, soot, and odor. God needs us — but not too much of us — and what He can use of us needs to be submerged in the Holy Spirit at all times.

The priests also kept the table of shewbread stocked at all times. Today's Church needs the presence of God's Spirit (light), but it also needs an abundance of God's Word (the bread). We priests must always keep the table of fellowship stocked with the bread of Christ's presence. Furthermore, when the priest was in the Holy Place, he burned incense upon the Golden Altar as the highest expression of worship that was available in the Tabernacle in the wilderness. The Levites with their musical instruments in the outer court did not represent the people in worship. That was done by the priest who burned the incense at the Golden Altar. Pastor-priests must become deeply involved in the worship expression of the local congregations, for they have access to the incense of worship. Delegating this responsibility to the musicians or a worship leader is expecting a Levite in the outer court to substitute for an Aaronic priest burning incense in the Holy Place. It won't work.

Another ministry given by God to the priests was the teaching of the Law. "The LORD spoke to Aaron, saying: '... teach the children of Israel all the statutes which the LORD has spoken to them by the hand of

Moses' '' (Leviticus 10:8, 11). Thank God for giving us teaching priests, for it is dangerous to assume that people know God's Word; it must be taught again and again. The priest is looked upon as the expert in the Word of God. He must know and show others the ways of God. He must preach and teach God's written Word. If the priest does not teach the Word of God, who will? The world, the flesh, and the devil certainly will not. God never planned that knowing His Word would be a self-taught project. He provided teachers for His people.

A sixth ministry that was reserved for the priesthood was being channels through which others could inquire of the Lord. Through the use of the *Urim* and *Thummim*, the high priest could discover God's will. We don't know just how it worked, but it seemed to be inerrant for Israel. Furthermore, through the use of the ephod, lesser priests could inquire of the Lord (*see* 1 Samuel 23:9, 10). God did not want His people to be unaware of His will and ways, so He chose certain persons, called "priests," to whom He could reveal His will. Believers have a right to expect their pastor-priests to help them find the mind and will of God. We priests have the gifts of the Spirit to help us; we have the indwelling Spirit to instruct us; and, according to Paul, "We have the mind of Christ" (1 Corinthians 2:16).

The Dynamic of the Priesthood

Hosea stated the obvious, "So it becomes — like priest, like people" (Hosea 4:9, Modern Language Version), for leader and follower end up at the same place. A priest can mold his people to become like himself, for when the priest believes and practices what he teaches, the people follow his example. Whether we like it or not, the spiritual life of a congregation is set by the priest, not by the people. How great, then, is the responsibility of the priesthood. In the economy of God, the spiritual life of a church will not rise above that of its priest. A praying priest will produce praying people; a praising and worshipping priest will have a congregation that will joyously respond to God; while a loving priest will produce a loving people. It is not so much that God sends in people who are like the priest; it is that the life of the priest changes the attitude of the people. John, in speaking of Christ, said, "As He is, so are we in this world" (1 John 4:17). Even so, as we the priests are, so are the people in our churches.

The Old Testament priest lived off his ministry. He ate portions of the sacrifices, and his inheritance came from the people he served. He was constantly a partaker of what he ministered. It is equally true with twentieth-century priests. We must be content to share the provisions of our people and accept that our inheritance on this earth will come from their provision. We must not only offer sacrifices for the people, we must be a partaker in those sacrifices. We must eat what we serve, for God has not made any other provisions for priests. We must control our "need-greed" level and not set our lifestyle too far above those we serve. A Cheverolet congregation finds it hard to understand why their priest needs a Mercedes, and so does God. We priests need to be content with those things that are provided for us rather than demand that we receive greater remuneration for our services than the people we serve receive for their work. Commonality serves communion.

Prayer:

Dear Jesus, the people I serve will never know You more intimately than I am able to present You to them. Please help me, for I feel so very inadequate. Show me how to bring people to You so that they may enjoy the life that You bring and love the Father Whom You represent. When I fail, correct me; when I falter, undergird me; and when I succeed, accept my praise and thanksgiving. Amen!

Chapter 5

Leaders as Potentates

"[He] has made us kings ... to His God and Father"
(Revelation 1:6)

Potentate is a strong word seldom used in modern English, but it is a scriptural word. Paul chose it when, in his exaltation of the majesty of our Lord Jesus Christ, he wrote, "He who is the blessed and only potentate, the King of kings and Lord of lords" (1 Timothy 1:15).

Perhaps this word is too lofty to be applied to ministers, for it implies supremacy of rulership, and yet there is a sense in which ministers, especially pastors, are viewed as the spiritual authority in their local congregations — they reign as kings. Whether sarcastically or seriously, Paul wrote to the leaders of the Corinthian church, "You have reigned as kings" (1 Corinthians 4:8). The twenty-four elders seated on thrones that surrounded God's throne sang, "[You] have made us kings ... to our God" (Revelation 5:10).

Even before God gave Israel the Law carved on the

two tablets of stone, He spoke through Moses to tell the people, "If you will indeed obey my voice and keep my covenant, then you shall be a special treasure to Me above all people ... and you shall be to Me a kingdom of priests and a holy nation" (Exodus 19:5, 6). God chose the nation to be priests unto Himself, but in the implementation of this He appointed Aaron and his sons to the office of priesthood and gave them the tribe of Levi as priestly representatives of the people.

When Peter wrote his first epistle he declared, "You are a chosen generation, a royal priesthood, a holy nation, His own special people, that you may proclaim the praises of Him who called you" (1 Peter 2:9). Such a declaration brings the commission of kingship and priesthood out of the future tense into the present tense, while the declaration of the elders in heaven put it in the present perfect tense: "You have made us kings" [Greek:"Co-regents"].

God purposed that we should reign with Him, provided that we should reign with Him, and proclaims that we now "... are a royal priesthood." This is beyond dispute. Whether God has implemented this by actually appointing every believer to kingship, or whether, as in the Old Testament provision, He chooses from among us those who will represent us in kingly ministries, may be open for debate. It does seem consistent with the New Testament teaching that while all believers share in the anointing of the Holy Spirit, God chooses some from among these anointed ones to place in offices of leadership (*see* Ephesians 4:11). Although the title *king* is not among the list of the five-fold ministries, each office unquestionably refers to authoritative leadership.

The Need for Authoritative Leadership

At least three times the Book of Judges records, "In those days there was no king in Israel" (*see* Judges 17:6;

18:1; 19:1), and twice adds, "Everyone did what was right in his own eyes" (Judges 17:6; 21:25). Even a cursory reading of this book will reveal that it was a time of lawlessness and repeated captivity for Israel. Although the Hebrews were both more numerous and far stronger than the enemy remnant left in the land, the lack of central leadership kept the tribes from working together against their common enemy. As a result, the enemy used the "divide and conquer" technique to harass and enslave the tribes of Israel.

From time to time, God would raise up a deliverer in the form of a judge, and the oppressor would be driven off for the lifetime of that judge. Other than Jephthah, none of these judges evidenced outstanding ability as a warrior, but the inspired leadership each offered united the people into action that brought them victory.

Human nature has not changed. United action still demands authoritative leadership. Quite consistently, the difference between a strong, growing church and a weak, defeated congregation is the pastor of each. The ability to inspire faith and action in others is essential in any ministry, but it is an absolute necessity in a pastor.

On many occasions, I have been called into a troubled church situation to act as a mediator and have found that usually the root of the problem was indecisive and weak leadership. People want and need authoritative leadership, whether it is offered under the Old Testament offices of prophet, priest, king, or judge, or under the New Testament offices of apostle, prophet, evangelist, pastor or teacher.

Ideally, the Church should function under the theocratic leadership of Christ the King, but practically, Christians need the guidance of human leaders as much as Israel needed Moses, Joshua, or David to unite them under the leadership of God. Perhaps this is why Jesus is called the "King of kings" (Revelation 19:16) and why Christian leaders are called "co-regents unto His God" (Revelation 1:6).

As long as Christ reigns over these lesser kings in the Church, they can serve a useful purpose and meet a need, for people without strong leaders are like sheep without a shepherd. Both groups are easily harmed by predators when they lack the protection of a leader. May God appoint us more men and women who will give us authoritative leadership under Christ!

Biblical Requirements for Authoritative Leaders

On Mount Sinai, God spoke to Moses and told him, "When you come to the land which the Lord your God is giving you, and possess it, and say 'I will set a king over me like all the nations that are round me,' you shall surely set a king over you whom the LORD your God chooses; one from among your brethren you shall set as king over you" (Deuteronomy 17:14,15). God foresaw that a pure theocracy would be rejected in favor of a monarchy, so He laid out requirements a king must meet to be acceptable to the Lord.

First, a king had to be one of the covenant people — a child of God, if you please. God never accepts an educated sinner as an authoritative leader over His chosen people. God's second requirement prohibited the king from setting a standard of living for himself that was excessively above the lifestyle of his people. The king was commanded to refrain from multiplying horses, wives, silver, or gold for his own use (*see* Deuteronomy 17:16, 17). The New Testament provision for spiritual leaders is very similar. Like Joseph of old, Israel's king was expected to gather wealth during times of plenty in order to be able to distribute it to the people during times of penury. Similarly, a minister receives to share, not hoard.

Third, the king was to guard against anything that would lift his heart in pride, for his appointment came from God and was not the result of any inherent goodness or ability he possessed (*see* Deuteronomy 17:20). No minister has an honest basis for pride, for he is but a servant of God to God's people.

Finally, God told Moses, "When he sits on the throne of his kingdom, that he shall write for himself a copy of this law in a book ... and it shall be with him, and he shall read it all the days of his life, that he may learn to fear the LORD his God and be careful to observe all the words of this law and these statutes" (Deuteronomy 17:18-19). God's authoritative leaders are required to write (or at least possess) a copy of God's Word, read it, and obey it in their day-to-day living. There can be no substitute for this rule.

Out of this standard of personal behavior God could expect just judgement, righteous instruction, and victorious battling from Israel's leaders. The New Testament requirements for authoritative leadership are but an expansion of these Old Testament commandments. In his pastoral epistles, Paul taught that leaders in God's Church must be blameless in their marriages and home management, be without greed or covetousness in their handling of finances, and be mature as Christians with good reputations in the community (*see* 1 Timothy 3:1-7). Leaders should not be learners who are practicing on people; they must be mature and seasoned Christians who have already learned how to put Bible principles into practical applications for everyday living.

How much damage has been done in the body of Christ by allowing immature students to ascend the throne of kingly leadership when they should have been under strong leadership themselves. As a punishment to Judah, the Lord told the prophet Isaiah, " '... I will give children to be their princes, and babes shall rule over them. The people will be oppressed' " (Isaiah 3:4-5). Leadership by the immature usually brings oppression to the Church. Solomon wisely said, "Woe to you, O Land, when your king is a child" (Ecclesiastes 10:16).

A few years ago, I was honored to be asked to present the graduation address at a major Bible college in the East. At the end of my prepared address to the largest graduating class in the school's history, I heard myself ad-libbing, "Now that you have learned everything this erudite faculty has been able to teach you, for God's sake, for the Church's sake, and for your own sake, do not immediately enter full-time Christian service. Most of you came directly from high school to this Bible school, and you have not yet learned how to live responsibly in this world. Go out and get jobs. Learn how to handle money and how to relate to people outside your religious walls. Then, when you have matured as people, let God call you into leadership in His Church."

My remarks were not only unexpected; they proved to be unacceptable to the faculty, who felt that these graduates were now ready to pastor any church in the nation. But absorbed facts cannot substitute for maturity that is produced through experience. God's authoritative leaders need to be persons of maturity, stature, experience, and compassion.

The Authoritative Leader in the Eyes of God

No matter how humble we may try to be, there still seems to be something "glamorous" about being a king in God's service. But we dare not lose sight of the fact that this office carries with it a tremendous weight of responsibility. The Old Testament kings were seen as God's agents, and God held them accountable for the spiritual condition of the land. We read that on several occasions when a king was unduly wicked, the Lord slew him. Even godly King Uzziah was smitten with leprosy by God's hand when he violated the Law and usurped the priesthood by entering the Holy Place to burn incense on the Golden Altar.

One of the extremely sobering truths of the book of Revelation is that Christ held the authoritative leader of each of the churches in Asia completely responsible for the spiritual condition of his local church. Every letter is addressed "to the angel of the church of ..." God would certainly have no occasion to write a letter through human agency to the angels who stand before His Throne, for He is on good speaking terms with His angels; He was addressing the local church leaders. To these leaders He declared, " 'I have this against you ... I know your works ... I have a few things against you ... repent, or else I will come to you quickly ...' " (Revelation 2:4, 9, 14, 16).

We who accept the kingly scepter need to remember that we reign *with* God, not *for* Him. Ours is a conferred and conditional authority, not an inherent and unlimited one. At best we are only the "assistant pastor." We do not govern under the Divine right of kings; we are appointees under the King of kings, and our appointment can be revoked as easily as our president can recall an ambassador from a foreign country.

It is a delight to be a co-regent in God's Kingdom, but it ever remains *His* Kingdom, and He insists that it be governed by His laws and ruled according to His will. All attempts to break free from God's rule in order to establish personal kingdoms are treated as insurrection and will meet God's righteous resistance and chastisement or even His severe judgment. How true it is that "the king's heart is in the hand of the LORD" (Proverbs 21:1).

The Authoritative Leader in the Eyes of the People

Although people need authoritative leadership, the nature of that leader, whether king or shepherd, and the manner in which he leads, makes a tremendous difference in the quality of the lives of those under his leadership. The Bible tells us that "when the righteous are in authority, the people rejoice; but when a wicked man rules, the people groan" (Proverbs 29:2). This is true whether the leader holds a national political office or is merely the pastor of a rural congregation. The peace or turbulence of the people is keyed to the manner in which they are governed.

Wise King Solomon observed, "The king who judges the poor with truth, his throne will be established forever" (Proverbs 29:14). What a tragedy it was that his son Rehoboam did not heed his father's words and because of his authoritarian harshness, lost ten of the twelve tribes over which his father had reigned.

Occasionally we read or hear of a loving pastor who devoted his entire ministry to a single congregation, but far more frequently we hear of pastors who have been asked to resign or who have caused splits in local congregations. We may be kings, but historically it has been repeatedly demonstrated that we have no more authority than people choose to grant to us. When we attempt to exceed this limit, they revolt and choose another king to reign over them. Whether or not their reasons or actions are equitable, this exists as an option, and a wise leader pays attention to the way he is viewed by his people.

The Authoritative Leader in His Own Eyes

Most persons accept a position of authoritative leadership with humility and a deep sense of personal inadequacy. It is likely that at one time or another each of us has explained to God that He made a mistake in calling us into His ministry. However, when this ministry is received and people applaud our leadership, we face a strong temptation to believe their adulation and to begin to enjoy the power of our position.

Repeatedly, we have witnessed the election or appointment of a local pastor to a state or national office in his denomination, and as he became comfortable with the inherent power of that office, he often began to exercise leadership over the very persons who placed him in that office. Somehow, the office seems to control the man rather than the man controlling the office. Power is infectious and can become a disease. Few seem to be immune. Jesus told His disciples, " 'You know that those who are considered rulers over the Gentiles lord it over them, and their great ones exercise authority over them. Yet it shall not be so among you; but whoever desires to become great among you shall be your servant' " (Mark 10:42, 43). *Positionally* we may be kings unto God, but *conceptually* we are servants to God's people. When this order gets reversed and we consider ourselves as kings who must be served by the people, we are already headed for trouble with God.

Rather than pride ourselves in our authority, we should constantly remind ourselves that we are under authority, for all rulers should also be ruled. The Roman centurion who asked Jesus to speak a healing word for his servant said, " 'I also am a man under authority, having soldiers under me' " (Matthew 8:9). Being *under* authority is an early qualification for being *in* authority, and we certainly cannot expect any more submission to our leadership than we are personally giving to Christ's leadership. The call to our people should be: "Follow me as I follow Christ."

We who have accepted the mantle of authoritative leadership under God must never forget how vitally we affect the lives of the people under us. God's Word says, "Where the word of a king is, there is power" (Ecclesiastes 8:4). We dare not play with people as pawns in a spiritual chess game, for our leadership will have an eternal impact upon many of these people.

Ours is a serious position that deeply affects the very ones for whom Christ died. They are not ours to use and abuse; they have been given to us so that we may lead them into the presence of Jesus as worshipping lovers of God.

It is likely that co-regents with God experience more difficulty with self-rule than with rule of the people of God. The Bible says, "He who rules his spirit [is better] than he who takes a city" (Proverbs 16:32). The person who has himself or herself under control is probably a candidate for leadership, but the individual whose home, finances, marriage, or morals are out of control has already forfeited all rights to the leadership of others.

In the Church, the rules that are good for the people must be equally good for their leader. The lifestyle prescribed for the congregation must also become the lifestyle of the pastor. If the people are expected to read the Bible and pray regularly, their leader must set the example. If the pastor challenges the people to give, he must certainly lead the way by his own giving.

Those leaders who seek to set themselves above the very principles they teach will live with gnawing guilt and an inner awareness that God will eventually hold them accountable for this double standard. We must remember that David got himself into trouble with God over Bathsheba because of his nonparticipation in the war into which he had sent his people. Our sitting back as nonparticipants while ordering others into action will always invite personal trouble. Kings are expected to lead the people; they don't merely shout orders like an excited child in a lively playground game.

An act of God has made us kings and priests unto Him, but our personal actions determine what kind of king we will be. We may set double standards, or we may live what we preach. If we govern ourselves by the same rules we apply to others, we will be respected by the people, honored by God, and loved by our families. If we do not, we will not even maintain self-respect.

A king is a king in all places and at all times. He has no office hours, nor does laying down his scepter make him a commoner. Every moment, even while on vacation, he represents the authority of the kingdom. No wonder Paul cried, "Who is sufficient for these things?" (2 Corinthians 2:16). But Paul also knew the answer, and it is ours as well: "Our sufficiency is from God, who also made us sufficient as ministers of the new covenant" (2 Corinthians 3:5, 6).

Kings, in their misguided sense of self-importance, tend to become a law unto themselves and place themselves above the very rules they enforce in others. When this happens in a Christian leader, his or her ministry is discredited by society and often becomes the basis for sensational news stories. Spiritual kings should learn to eat what they serve. God does not have double standards; one law fits all.

Prayer:

Dear Lord Jesus, please help me to hold the scepter of authority very carefully. Help me keep rightly related to You so I will not be tempted to play "lord" with Your chosen people. Help me guard my thoughts and attitudes so that I need not fear my words and actions. Forever remind me that I am only reigning with You and that You will show me how to do what You want me to do. Amen!

Chapter 6

Leaders as Prodigals

"Father, give me my share of the estate"
(Luke 15:12, NIV)

Few of Christ's parables are better known than the one we call "The Prodigal Son." The younger of two sons was apparently tired of working with the father in farming and requested his inheritance long before his father's death. He took his substance with him as he journeyed into another part of the world. We're all familiar with what happened to him from that point on.

This story has formed the basis of many evangelistic sermons and it has been the tool for bringing wandering Christians back to the loving Father's house. There is, however, another application that is equally valid, since the story concerns a father, a farm, and servant-sons who work with the father. If we see God as the Father, the world as the farm, and ministers of the Gospel as the servant-sons, we may very well see ourselves in the picture.

Whether we serve as prophets, priests, or kings, we are still but servant-sons working with the heavenly Father on His farm, the earth. We use His tools, follow His methods, plant the crops of His bidding, and receive His providential care. For a season it seems good to us, but individualism, pride, and even greed often cause us to seek to improve on God's methods. Rather than continue to do things as they have been done for generations, we want to strike out on our own and make a fortune our way. Accordingly, we ask for an early settlement of our inheritance and leave the homestead to show Father and the elder brother that we can do better with our methods than they can do with their outdated ways.

It is not incidental that Jesus said that it was the "younger son" who made this demand, for it is characteristic of youth to want to try their wings. There is a place for this, for without innovation the church would be locked into sameness, but if the new way takes us off of the Father's farm and away from His presence, the result will be predictable. Many ministers have tried to survive by eating with the hogs, but eventually their better sense convinced them to humble themselves and return to the Father.

Prodigal Prophets

The life of a prophet is very circumscribed, and he exercises no control over his message. The people to whom he speaks are rarely appreciative, and are often outright hostile. When called upon to give the Word of the Lord, he is often primed by the recipients and made to understand just what they want to hear. If he does not say what their ears are listening for, he is either ignored or punished. Prophets soon learn that their form of "farming" with the Father is hard work with a minimum of reward. The pressure of desiring to be accepted plus the need to be provided for has caused many prophets both in Bible times and modern days to launch out on their own, taking the Father's inheritance with them.

Perhaps the book of Jeremiah speaks to this improvident use of the prophetic office more forcefully than any. To and through Jeremiah, God spoke again and again of the gross misuse of the prophetic calling. " 'Behold, I am against the prophets,' says the LORD, 'who use their tongues and say, "He says." ' " (Jeremiah 23:31). What a temptation it is to put God's name on our thoughts, plans, and programs when presenting them to the people, for most people will respond favorably to "a Word from the Lord." I have long yearned to hear God speak through a prophet and say, "I did not say that" after listening to one of the wild, off-the-wall prophecies that were given as a "Thus saith the Lord." The way we make God responsible for some of the nonsense that comes right out of our own minds is nothing short of criminal.

Again God said, " 'The prophets prophesy lies in my name. I have not sent them, commanded them, nor spoken to them; they prophesy to you a false vision, divination, a worthless thing, and the deceit of their heart' " (Jeremiah 14:14). Throughout all ages, when God has sent a prophet among His people, there have arisen self-appointed persons who sense in God's chosen man the flow of anointing and the acceptance that comes to him, and they emulate his style and ingratiate themselves to the hungry people of God. They have no relationship with God, but they purpose to speak on His behalf and end up deceiving and destroying the very people Christ died to redeem and restore to fellowship with the Father.

Wantonness in ministry will breed wantonness in behavior. It is almost to be expected that if a person will lie about being God's messenger, he will be deceitful in other things. God said, " 'I have seen a horrible thing in the prophets of Jerusalem: they commit adultery and walk in lies' " (Jeremiah 13:14). These lead others not only into false messages, but into failing morals as well. If we will distort the Father's inheritance for acceptance, what is to prevent us from distorting it to satisfy our carnal cravings?

Lying, deceit, pretence, and adulterous living by prophets are but outer manifestations of an inner rebellion. These prophets have left the Father, His farm, and His procedure to set up their own business with their inheritance. It is doomed to failure from the very start, but that collapse will hurt many innocent Christians. The prodigal prophet can be restored to fellowship with the Father by returning with a repentant heart, but what about the many persons to whom he deceitfully represented the will and Word of the Father?

Prodigal Priests

Many of the built-in negatives in the role of a prophet are lacking in the role of the priest. The priestly office carries a sanctity with it. God made ample provision for their livelihood, and there was a protective brotherhood in their way of service. Still, the Scriptures speak of many prodigals in the priesthood, and their departure from the ways of the Father Who set them in office seems to fall into one of four categories.

Perhaps the most obvious of these was the *commercialization* of the priesthood. God made ample provision for His priests. Since He had taken the Levites in place of Israel's firstborn, He provided that the priests be supported by all of Israel. The tithes of the people were used for this support. Although the priests were never numbered with Israel and had no inheritance in the land, they were given six cities in which to live. Furthermore, God made provision for the priests to eat a portion of the sacrifices brought as acts of worship. In spite of all of this, Levi's sons despised God's provision and made their own demands, insisting on the right to choose the part of the sacrifice they wanted (often taking it before the sacrifice was ever offered to the Lord). Like the young prodigal, they could not be content with the Father's provision.

In Judges 18, we read that Micah actually hired a young Levite to become his household priest so that, instead of going to the Tabernacle for acts of worship, he could stay right in his own yard to do them. Later this priest was captured by the small army of Dan, who made him a tribal priest. The priesthood that had once exclusively served God was now available for hire.

The prophet Micah lamented the commercialization of the priesthood: "Her priests teach for pay, and her prophets divine for money. Yet they lean on the LORD, and say, 'Is not the LORD among us? No harm can come upon us' " (Micah 3:11). How we could wish that this merchandising of the priest's office ended with the close of the Old Testament, but it is still with us. Perhaps we will always have those among us who, for a fee, will presume to offer the rituals of our God on our behalf, but when a prophet or priest is in the employ of the people to whom they minister, their message is controlled by whoever signs the paycheck.

Another perversion in the priesthood was its *imperialization*. God observed, " 'An astonishing and horrible thing has been committed in the land: The prophets prophesy falsely, and the priests rule by their own power; and My people love to have it so. But what will you do in the end?' " (Jeremiah 5:30, 31). God established the priesthood to assist the people in their worship, not to establish an authoritarian rule over them; but the lust for power causes persons to parley a small measure of power into total control, and the priests were no exception. The priesthood was provided to enfold persons into God, not to enforce the priest's superiority upon the people. Priests were given authority with God, but not over people; nonetheless, by the time of Christ, the priests were the dominant power over the people. The priests condemned Jesus to death and the Apostles to imprisonment. Instead of bringing people to God, they were using their titular position with God to dominate the lives of people. Actually, using spiritual power to dominate and control people is viewed as witchcraft in the Bible. The imperialization of the priesthood not only went beyond God's provisions, it defied His prohibitions. God separated the offices of king and priest. When the priest insists upon being king, the land is left without a priest.

A third way the priests showed themselves to be prodigal was in their violation of the Law. One of the causes for the capture of Judah by the Babylonians was the priests' violation of the very Law they had been commissioned to teach. God said, " 'Her priests have violated My law and profaned My holy things; they have not distinguished between the holy and unholy, nor have they made known the difference between the unclean and the clean; and they have hidden their eyes from My Sabbaths, so that I am profaned among them' " (Ezekiel 22:26), and the prophet Zephaniah declared, "Her priests have polluted the sanctuary, they have done violence to the law" (Zephaniah 3:4).

It is self-evident that if the priest does not practice what he teaches, then no one will live God's Word. Yet the Levites were not the only priests to twist the law to excuse performance that is in violation of the Law of God. Today's priests can give an interpretation of God's Word that authorizes any excess or sin in which they may be involved. Knowledge of the Law encourages the formation of loopholes.

As serious as this is, the worst violation of the Law is the abandoning of the Law. God's message was, " 'My people are destroyed for lack of knowledge. Because you have rejected knowledge, I also will reject you from being priest for Me; because you have forgotten the law of your God, I also will forget your children' " (Hosea 4:6). Currently in America, we have so many substitutes for God's Word that we end up abandoning that Word. We push programs, projects, people, and provision for needs. We talk doctrine, dreams, desires, and differences, but where is God's Word? Is it remotely possible that the loss of a priest's children to the ways of God is a result of abandoning the Law in the home and private life of the priest? For God did say, " 'Because you have forgotten the law of your God, I also will forget your children.' "

In the final book of the Old Testament, God lamented, " 'A son honors his father, and a servant his master. If then I am the Father, where is My honor? And if I am a Master, where is My reverence? Says the LORD of hosts to you priests who despise My name' " (Malachi 1:6). The verses that follow define what God means by "despising His name." They speak of offering defiled food on the altar and of offering blind, lame, and sick animals as sacrifices. God demanded the best as offerings unto Himself, and they were substituting the very worst.

Whenever we give God less than the best, we too have despised His name. We are often so busy honoring one another that we don't get around to honoring God. Our public praying seldom evidences advance thinking or deep feeling. We extemporize words without bothering to have thoughts, and even the way we serve Communion often borders on disrespect.

The prodigal teachers of the Law became persistent violators of that Law both in precept and in principle. It is no great surprise, then, that they also got involved in immorality with the worshippers. This is the sin that caused God to wrest leadership from Eli's priesthood and give it to the prophet Samuel. Eli did not restrain his "staff" (his sons) from taking sexual advantage of the women worshippers.

Priests soon learn that worshippers are vulnerable to sexual advances. Some scientists declare that the portion of our brain that gets involved with worship is adjacent to the portion that controls our sex drive, and one signal can "bleed over" into the other segment of the mind. Throughout history, religious practices and immorality have gone hand in hand, even to the institution of prostitution as an act of worship. In helping people to worship, we assist them in opening their emotions to express love and adoration. A simple redirecting of these same expressions puts them at the disposal of the priest. Psychologically, a priest taking sexual advantage of a worshipper is akin to incest with the father. Once again, a trusted authority figure violates personal morality, and few experiences in life can damage a woman more than incest, whether it be family or priest. Nothing can mar worship relationships faster than this. Prodigal priests may be having their fun, but they are destroying the very people they were commissioned to serve.

A fourth way priests can show their prodigal nature is in misdirecting worship by leading people to worship the wrong object. God said, " 'The Levites who went far from Me, when Israel went astray, who strayed away from Me after their idols, they shall bear their iniquity' " (Ezekiel 44:10). Idols may be metal or mental, but they are still something short of God Himself. It may seem expedient to direct people's devotion to the American dream that has been Christianized, or to structure, doctrine, practice, or even other people, but it fast becomes idolatry, for it is a replacement of God as the object of our affections.

Very early in the priesthood God had to command, " 'They [the priests] shall no more offer their sacrifices

to demons, after whom they have played the harlot' "
(Leviticus 17:7). How tragic that persons ordained by
God to lead people into Divine worship would actually
lead people in the worship of demons; but it can be done
so insidiously that we are unaware of it until the
consequences are upon us. Simply directing too much
of people's attention to the demonic can become a
worship of demons. Making all negatives the work of
the devil will create a respect for the devil that becomes
worship. Satan wants our reverential attention, and
priests who are trying to find a way other than the
Father's way often fall into the trap of continually
calling people's attention to the demonic. This, to the
spirit world, is acceptable worship.

Prodigal Kings

Obviously there are prodigal failures in the priesthood, but there are equal failures in the kings. The very
first king, Saul, gave God only partial obedience and
spared the best of the persons and animals God commanded him to utterly destroy. He thought that he
knew more than God, just as the younger son thought
he knew more than his father. Solomon, so loved by
God and so endowed with wisdom from God, ignored
God's prohibition of having multiple wives and acquired
1,000 wives and concubines. In the end, these wives
turned his heart away from Jehovah.

When the kingdom split under Rehoboam, Uzziah, a
godly king of Judah, sought to usurp the office of the
priesthood by burning incense upon the Golden Altar,
and God smote him with leprosy. Hezekiah, another
righteous king in Judah, flagrantly displayed all of his
wealth to the ambassadors of Babylon, thereby creating
a lust in Babylon's king that eventually led to the
capture of Judah. These were good men and outstand-
ingly qualified kings, but, somewhere in the exercise of

their powers, they placed themselves above the commands of God.

Jeroboam quickly led the ten tribes of Israel into idolatry by making the two golden calves as a substitute for God's tabernacle, and the succession of nineteen kings that followed him give us no examples of great godliness.

Perhaps none of us is exempt from taking the office God has entrusted to us and using it for our own advantage rather than for the building and establishing of the Kingdom of God. When we do so, we waste what God gave to us and we injure those to whom we minister. Our only redemption is to return to the Father and humbly ask His forgiveness and restoration. He is already waiting with a ring, a robe, and a kiss; and as soon as we are cleaned up from the mess into which we got ourselves by leaving His will in the first place, the banquet will begin.

The prodigal principle can work in any realm of leadership God may entrust to us. These have but been illustrative. God's work must be done by God's man in God's way. Anytime we seek to improve on God's methods and invest God's goods in human endeavors, we can expect to end in the pig-pen, completely stripped of everything that God entrusted to us. Our very survival depends upon a humble return to the Father with an honest confession: "I have sinned, and am no longer worthy...." The Father's forgiveness and restoration enable us to return to the banqueting table to eat what we serve.

Prayer:

Dear Jesus, my heart is just as prone to depart from You as was the heart of any of these prophets, priests, or kings. Please extend abundant mercy to me and keep a tight reign upon my life. When I ask for "the portion of goods that belongs to me," please don't give it to me. Make me stay on Your farm and work with You and my Elder Brother, for this is my deep desire. Ignore the crying of my flesh and listen to the crying of my heart. I want You and Your provisions more than anything else in life. This desire has come from You, so honor it at all times. My desires are transient and beggarly; Your desires are eternal and sumptuous. Thank You for keeping me in the center of Your will, for I do not have enough years left in my life to play the role of the wandering prodigal. Thank You for this grace. Amen!

Chapter 7

Leaders as Pastors

"A pastor to follow thee" (Jeremiah 17:16, KJV)

I am convinced that the greatest gift God can give to a local congregation, after Jesus, is a true pastor. In our complex society, people are confused, and they need a pastor to teach them how to relate to life. Many Christians are deeply hurt and need a pastor to bring healing to their emotions, while others have lost their way in our amoral society and need a pastor to guide them back to biblical standards. Our nearly wholesale embracing of divorce has left us with a generation of lonely people of all ages who need a pastor to befriend them and to help them establish other friendships in the Christian community.

No government agency can fill the role of a pastor, nor can educational or cultural institutions meet the needs of the human heart as quickly and as permanently as a pastor. Those persons who have established a relationship with a pastor in a local congregation find a security that no insurance company could ever provide.

It is the pastor who shares life's most important and traumatic events. He marries the living and buries the dead. He visits the sick and comforts the afflicted. He dedicates the babies, provides for the religious instruction of the children, gives guidance to the young people, counsels the young marrieds, and visits the aged. All the while, he functions as the head of a religious corporation that maintains facilities and services for the entire community.

Some people worship the very ground he walks on, while others are jealous and fearful of him. He is both hero and villain who can either do no wrong or no right, depending upon a person's current relationship to him. Sometimes he is pictured as a demagogue; other times as a demigod, but he is necessary for Christian maturity, for he is the resident office of the five-fold ministries.

Although the term *pastor* is an extremely common and endearing term used in the Christian community for our spiritual leader, it is not a common Bible word. The New King James version of the Bible uses the word *pastor* only once — in listing the five ministerial offices of "apostles, prophets, evangelists, pastors and teachers" (Ephesians 4:11). The Greek word that is translated "pastors" here is *poimen*, which means "a shepherd." The equivalent Hebrew word is *ra'ah*. Jeremiah used this word eight times when speaking of those persons appointed of God to give spiritual guidance to His people. While it literally means "to tend, to pasture, to graze a flock," by extension, it means to rule [the flock] or to shepherd them. The New King James Bible translates *ra'ah* as "rulers" three times and as "shepherds" five times.

The Pastor's Role

When Paul bade farewell to the Ephesian elders at Miletus, he used three distinct titles for men who are selected by God to lead a congregation: *elders, overseers, shepherds* (*see* Acts 20:17, 28). These titles give us some insight into the nature of their responsibilities. In speaking of "elders," the Greek word Paul used is *presbuterious.* It denoted mature men who were known for their expedience and wisdom. While in some segments of the Body of Christ this word has become the title of a religious office, in the Bible it is used to signify the kind of person the pastor should be. It deals more with the pastor's character than with his calling. It prescribes qualities of spiritual maturity and depth.

When Paul also spoke of pastors being overseers, he chose the Greek word *episkopas,* which refers to one who supervised and directed workmen in the performance of their duties. It is the root for the English word *bishop.* Whereas *presbyter* referred to the pastor's character, *overseer* referred primarily to the nature of the pastor's work. It indicated his administrative function.

The third term Paul employed is *poimmainein,* or "shepherd." Perhaps, more than the other two words, it speaks of the spirit in which the pastor performs his work. The pastor is a shepherd who realizes that he works with living beings, not with cold statistics. Pastoring is not a mechanical care, it is a loving concern. As the shepherd, the pastor is so involved with the sheep that their well-being has the highest priority in his life.

The Pastor's Resolve

The pastor who enlists in the service of the Lord for a tour of duty is self-deceived, for, unlike the U.S. military service, God does not accept four-year enlistments. Pastoring is a life-time commitment. In listing the five-fold "ascension gifts," as these ministries are often called, Paul said that Christ gave us pastor-teachers "Till we all come in the unity of the faith, and of the knowledge of the Son of God, unto a perfect man, unto the measure of the stature of the fullness of

Christ" (Ephesians 4:13). As the sheep mature, they give birth to lambs that must be brought through the full life cycle of maturity. It is highly improbable that any pastor will succeed in bringing every member of his congregation to this level of faith, knowledge, perfection, and fullness of Christ, since all new converts start at square one. Happy is the pastor who realizes and accepts that his job is never completed. Goals may be achieved, but there will never be a time when the people do not need their pastor. Talk about job security!

All ministers are placed in the Body "for the equipping of the saints for the work of ministry, for the edifying of the body of Christ." (Ephesians 4:12). The *King James Version* says, "For the perfecting of the saints, for the work of the ministry, for the edifying of the body of Christ," while the *New International Version of the Bible* translates this: "To prepare God's people for work of service, so that the body of Christ may be built up." Pastors are Divinely placed in the Church to equip, perfect, or prepare God's people to function effectively in the sphere of ministry God has chosen for them.

Pastors are no more expected to do the work of ministry for the congregation than a shepherd is expected to grow wool, give birth to lambs, or provide mutton. Both of these leaders have the responsibility to care for their charges so that they are able to do what they were born (or born again) to do. Far too many churches function like a football team — eleven exhausted staff members on the playing field, and the grandstand filled with cheering but underexercised church members. Pastors are shepherds, not playing coaches. Our job is to get everyone involved in the work of the ministry. It is always better to get ten persons working than to try to do the work of ten people.

The Pastor's Responsibilities

In declaring Himself to be the good shepherd, Jesus taught some basic principles about pastoring and its responsibilities. He said that the shepherd "calls his own sheep by name and leads them out. And when he brings out his own sheep, he goes before them; and the sheep follow him, for they know his voice" (John 10:3)4). Obviously, then, the shepherd *leads* his flock. Since we can only lead if we are in motion, pastors must be moving on in God, breaking new ground, making spiritual progress as an example for the flock to follow. Our example must include our own family, for if we can't lead the mini-flock at home the Word disqualifies us from tending the larger flock in the local church (*see* 1 Timothy 3:4-5; Titus 1:6). The shepherd first, the flock second is Paul's order of responsibility: " 'Take heed to yourselves and to all the flock' " (Acts 20:28). What we are they will become; where we are, they will pasture; and where we lead they will follow. The pastor never drives the sheep; he always leads them by the power of his presence and example.

The pastor, like the Good Shepherd, will also *serve* his people. Peter challenged the pastors, "Shepherd the flock of God ... serving ... willingly ... eagerly" (1 Peter 5:2). God's flock does not exist for the welfare of the pastors; the pastors are appointed to serve the welfare of the sheep. Whether that entails removing burrs from the wool, cleansing and sanitizing a wound, helping the ewes bear their lambs, shearing the heavy wool, or feeding and watering them, pastors serve the sheep as their first responsibility.

Pastors also *rule* the flock. It is interesting that the Greek word *rabdos*, "rule," means both the staff of the shepherd and the scepter of the ruler. Just as Moses' rod, or shepherd's staff, became the symbol of his leadership, so each pastor has a staff that means "the buck stops here." The shepherd's rule, however, is not heavy-handed authoritarianism, for when Peter urged the elders to oversee the sheep, he quickly added, "Not as being lords over those entrusted to you" (1 Peter 5:3). Actually, the rule of a shepherd isn't even connected with an office, for the Greek word *archein*, meaning "to rule" in the hierarchal sense, is never used of Christian leaders. The rule of a shepherd is like that of a loving father over his children. He uses his authority to build up, not to pull down. He rules by example, by giving a lead, by decision-making, and by resolving issues.

Perhaps the most obvious responsibility of a pastor is to *feed the people*. This is the teaching function of a pastor, and "a servant of the Lord must ... be ... able to teach" (2 Timothy 2:24). The shepherd must teach more than mere doctrinal concepts. Ultimately the shepherd must teach his people how to live. The flock does not need lectures on grass technology or the workings of a sheep's digestive system; they need to be taken to the green pastures and still waters, where they can eat and grow strong. The shepherd must be concerned with every aspect of the lives of the sheep, both natural and spiritual. The Bible has much to say on the so-called secular topics, for in Christ everything is spiritual. The sheep need to be taught how to live a well-rounded life in the here and now, not merely look forward to the sweet by and by. Furthermore, the godly shepherd ensures that his sheep not only look at the grass (receive teaching), but actually feed on that grass (put that teaching into practice).

The pastor-shepherd also *protects* his flock. After pastoring the church in Ephesus for three or more years, Paul handed over full responsibility of leadership to the elders. Foremost among his exhortations to them was, "Be on guard for yourselves and for all the flock" (Acts 20:28 NASV). Pagan influence and threats (*see*

Acts 19:23-41), heresy in the form of legalism (Judaizers) and super-spirituality (Gnostics), and, worst of all, disruptive influences within the church — wolves in sheep's clothing (*see* Acts 20:29-30) — were all dangers that the Ephesian shepherds were urged to spot and firmly deal with for the protection of the sheep. Amazingly, the situation remains unchanged today after all these hundreds of years.

The Pastors' Rebuke

In Christ's letters to the seven churches in Asia (Revelation 1:3), He holds the local pastor, whom He calls the "angel [messenger] of the church," totally responsible for the condition in the local church. The people are not threatened, but the pastor is. The way we handle our shepherding responsibilities determines the spiritual condition of the flock, and it will also establish the basis of God's dealing with the shepherd.

The weeping prophet, Jeremiah, received several rebuking messages from God about the shepherd pastors. The first was, "For the shepherds have become dull hearted, and have not sought the LORD; therefore they shall not prosper, and all their flocks shall be scattered" (Jeremiah 10:21). Because they continually face crises and turmoil in the lives of the members of their congregations, pastors quite frequently build defensive walls around themselves, causing them to become calloused and insensitive to the feelings of their people. A dull-hearted pastor — one who is unfeeling — cannot enter into the lives of his people; he can but function as a professional counsellor who has good concepts but no genuine concern. The *King James Version* translates this phrase, "For the shepherds have become brutish." It is sad when a pastor responds more as an animal than as a human. God has not chosen to lead His flock with a ram, but with a person. God wants and needs all of the sensitivity and alertness that people can bring into the task of shepherding God's flock.

It may well be argued that no person can carry the needs, burdens, problems, and inadequacies of an entire congregation of people, but God never intended that we carry these pressures any farther than the Divine presence. Every pressure of Israel was carried by Moses into God's presence for an answer to the problem. God told Jeremiah that the shepherds had become dull-hearted because they "have not sought the LORD." Our sensitivity will be maintained only as we regularly come into the presence of God, who is the true Shepherd over the flock of God. Pastors who will not regularly pray are told that "they shall not prosper, and all their flocks shall be scattered." Prayerlessness in a pastor is not merely criminal, it is fatal!

A second rebuke God gave to pastors through Jeremiah was, " 'Woe to the shepherds who destroy and scatter the sheep of My pasture!' says the LORD" (Jeremiah 23:1). God had earlier spoken of His leaders destroying His vineyard and portion, making His pleasant portion a desolate wilderness (*see* Jeremiah 12:10). God appoints shepherds or pastors not to destroy and scatter, but to gather and build. The sheep are not given for mutton and lamb chops; they are there to have lambs and to grow wool. Shepherds who use the flock for their own gain destroy what belongs to God, and they will have to face an irate and judgmental God. It is tragic how many sheep are scattered by ambitious pastors whose personal goals are more important to them than are the lives of the sheep.

A third major rebuke is an extension of the preceding two reprimands: "Therefore thus says the LORD God of Israel against the shepherds who feed My people: 'You have scattered My flock, driven them away, and not attended to them. Behold, I will attend to you for the evil of your doings,' says the LORD" (Jeremiah 23:2). "Scattered ... driven ... not attended." What an indictment. If God cannot entrust His sheep to His shepherds, to whom can He commit them? The world, the flesh, and the devil are out to destroy God's people. If the pastors join forces with them, the cry will again have to go out: "Who is on the Lord's side?" (Exodus 32:26, KJV).

Again and again, as pastors have become dull-hearted, self-seeking persons who scattered God's flock and destroyed His vineyard, God has had to raise up other shepherds to tend His sheep. God will not leave His sheep without a shepherd, but He does threaten to leave many shepherds without sheep.

The shepherd role should not be difficult for one who maintains his relationship to the Good Shepherd. We learn by observing. We can lead because we have become His followers. We never rise to a position higher than under-shepherd, so the ultimate responsibility remains with Christ. As long as we are eating in Christ's pasture it is easy to lead our little flock into that pasture. If we enjoy the clear, still waters of His provision, we know where to lead the people entrusted to our guidance for refreshing. A faithful shepherd of God's flock not only eats what he serves; he serves what he eats, and the flock is greatly benefited.

Prayer:

Dear Jesus, just as You told Peter that the test of his love for You would be to feed Your sheep, so You have called me to tend Your lambs. At the beginning, I was completely dedicated to this task and gave my life for the sheep, but as I get older and more experienced, I tend to get calloused and dull-hearted in dealing with the same problems and needs over and over again. I keep forgetting that it is not the same sheep who are having these problems. Forgive me for expecting the new lambs to automatically know and possess what I have taught and given to the older sheep. Please motivate me to seek Your face again and again until I regain the spiritual sensitivity I once possessed. And if I cannot again be filled with compassion and concern for Your flock, please remove me and give to these sheep one whose heart is tender, sensitive, and loving, for the sheep are far more valuable than I am. Amen!

Chapter 8

Leaders as Preachers

"Preach the Word" (2 Timothy 4:2)

In the United States, the word *preacher* has become a term covering everyone who is in full-time ministry. We use this word to denote a pastor, an evangelist, a television personality, a deacon, and even a minister of music. In the Bible, however, the term has a very specific and limited meaning. It denotes "one who proclaims publicly." It does not necessarily speak of an office, but it consistently speaks of an activity. King Solomon called himself a "preacher" (*see* Ecclesiastes 1:1), although he obviously was a king, and the prophets were often preachers without ever surrendering their prophetic office. Their proclamation, not their position, made preachers out of them.

It is obvious that graduation from a Bible college does not make a person a preacher, nor does subsequent ordination into the ministry. The public proclamation of Divine precepts produces a preacher.

A preacher is a communicator, a messenger, or an

interpreter of what God is saying. He hears God's word in his spirit and communicates it with his voice. He has developed sufficient skill to enable him to make others understand what is in his spirit. His message may exhort, excite, comfort, challenge, convict, or convert his hearers, but they cannot listen to him without a response. He has something to say, and he says it succinctly enough that his hearers understand his message.

The Place of Preaching

Not all ministry is preaching, but preaching is a God-ordained ministry of great importance. Twice Paul declared, "I was appointed a preacher, an apostle, and a teacher" (1 Timothy 2:7 and 2 Timothy 1:11). It is worth noting that both times Paul spoke of his appointment to preach before he mentioned his apostleship or his ministry of teaching, which may indicate the priority he placed on preaching.

As Apostle to the Gentiles, Paul had learned that missionary evangelism must precede pastoring or teaching, and he saw preaching as the key to that evangelism. It was he who asked these questions: "How shall they call on him in whom they have not believed? And how shall they believe in Him of Whom they have not heard? And how shall they hear without a preacher?" (Romans 10:14). The proclamation of preaching is a necessary prelude to the operation of faith, for "faith comes by hearing, and hearing by the word of God" (Romans 10:17).

In many of our American churches, preaching has been de-emphasized and almost replaced with the sacraments, musicals, programs, dramas, and even films. Perhaps it can be successfully argued that all of these proclaim a message, but man has yet to devise an acceptable substitute for good preaching. Heart-to-heart communication of God's love is the very core of the Gospel, which is "good news."

We live in a very troubled generation that has cast off restraints, mortgaged its future, and deified the individual. Sensuality and violence have replaced spiritual values and morality, and the anxiety and fear that have resulted were predictable. In a similar generation, God's word to the prophet was, " 'Comfort, yes, comfort My people!' Says your God. 'Speak comfort to Jerusalem ...' " (Isaiah 40:1). A more literal translation of the Hebrew word for "comfort" is "speak to the heart." God needs messengers who can speak heart-to-heart to people. Head-to-head communication cannot reach our generation. What is needed is a flow of Divine love — from one who is currently experiencing that love to someone who is hurting because of a lack of that love. This is the main mission of preaching.

God places a high priority upon preaching, for when Jesus came, "He began to preach" (Matthew 4:17). When He was invited to speak in the synagogue of His home town, He asked for the Isaiah scroll number two and read, " 'The Spirit of the LORD is upon Me, because He has anointed Me to preach the gospel to the poor. He has sent Me to heal the brokenhearted, to preach deliverance to the captives and recovery of sight to the blind, to set at liberty those who are oppressed, to preach the acceptable year of the LORD' " (Luke 4:18 quoted from Isaiah 61:1, 2). When He was aware that He had the full attention of those in the synagogue He added, " 'Today this Scripture is fulfilled in your hearing' " (Luke 4:21).

Three times Jesus said that He was anointed to *preach*, and how He preached! Even His enemies had to testify, " 'No man ever spoke like this Man!' " (John 7:46).

Jesus told His disciples, " 'Whatever I tell you in the dark, speak in the light; and what you hear in the ear, preach on the housetops' " (Matthew 10:27). He wanted more than disciples [learners]; He wanted preachers [proclaimers]. John later testified, "That which we have seen and heard we declare to you" (1 John 1:3).

Preaching is not a modern art. Before the Flood, "Noah was a preacher of righteousness" (2 Peter 2:5); Jonah was delivered from the large fish and was instructed, " 'Arise, go to Ninevah, that great city, and preach to it the message that I tell you' " (Jonah 3:2). Preaching has always been one of God's key tools for communicating His love and His Word to great numbers of people, and it works. Paul wrote, "It pleased God through the foolishness of preaching to save those who believed" (1 Corinthians 1:21, KJV), and he further testified, "We preach Christ crucified, to the Jews a stumbling block and to the Greeks foolishness ... but to those who are called, both Jews and Greeks, Christ the power of God and the wisdom of God" (1 Corinthians 12:23, 24).

Paul's instruction to Timothy was, "Preach the Word! Be ready in season and out of season. Convince, rebuke exhort, with all longsuffering and teaching" (2 Timothy 4:2). It would indeed be difficult to find a better definition of preaching, for preaching exhibits the power to persuade, the courage to confront, and the tenacity to teach with patience and gentleness. Its purpose goes beyond mere communication of a message; it seeks to effect changes in people because of that message. In fact, Paul believed that it would be difficult to overemphasize the place of preaching in the work of the Lord. He felt the call to preach so strongly that he cried out, "Yes, woe is me if I do not preach the gospel" (1 Corinthians 9:16).

The Person of the Preacher

Solomon, who began the book of Ecclesiastes by declaring himself a preacher, ended this book with some sound advice for preachers. He wrote, "And moreover, because the Preacher was wise, he still taught the people knowledge; yes, he pondered and sought out and set in order many proverbs. The Preacher sought to find acceptable words; and what was written was upright — words of truth. The words of the wise are like goads, and the words of scholars are like well-driven nails, given by one Shepherd" (Ecclesiastes 12:9-11).

In this passage, Solomon made three statements that particularly apply to the person of the preacher: Be wise; fear God; keep His Commandments. The need for wisdom was his first observation, for preachers do not necessarily need to be clever or brilliant, but they desperately need to be wise. Since few persons are inherently wise, the preacher is dependent upon an outside source of wisdom. Fortunately, the first manifestation of the Spirit is "the word of wisdom through the Spirit" (1 Corinthians 12:8), and we are further assured that " 'the fear of the Lord is the beginning of wisdom; and the knowledge of the Holy is understanding' " (Proverbs 9:10).

Real wisdom is a knowledge of Divine things, and this knowledge is the only stable foundation for a preaching ministry. Wisdom is available to the preacher, but he must seek it in the Spirit and in the Word. Consistent communion with God is required to maintain a flow of wisdom to share with people. As James said plainly, "If any of you lacks wisdom, let him ask of God, who gives to all liberally and without reproach, and it will be given him" (James 1:5). To declare, "Thus saith the Lord," without genuinely knowing what the Lord is saying is both deceitful and dangerous to the preacher as well as to the people.

Solomon brought his message to a close by urging, "Let us hear the conclusion of the whole matter: fear God and keep His commandments" (Ecclesiastes 12:13). Is there anyone in the ministry who needs to fear God more than the preacher does? Love for God must always be balanced with a fear of God. The preacher, who is so dependent upon God for his message and for the necessary wisdom to declare that message profitably, lives in a healthy fear of disobeying, despising, or displeasing God, for that would break the vital relationship with Him.

The Hebrew word Solomon choose for "fear" is *yaw-ray*, which literally means "to put in fear" or "to be afraid." We often translate it as "to revere" or "to reverence." The person who dares to publicly proclaim God's message needs a holy reverence for the God he represents. He dare not make God commonplace or ordinary, for God is holy, and His Words are holy words filled with the authority and power of His excellent nature. By those words, He created the earth, and His words have the power to recreate the lives of people today. Certainly the messenger of those majestic words must have a deep reverence for and fear of Him Who uttered them.

To the admonition to fear God, Solomon added the phrase "and keep His commandments" (Ecclesiastes 12:13). Preachers are more than mere messengers of God; they are also examples for the people to whom they preach. Repeatedly, God used the lives of His preaching prophets to reinforce the message they were delivering. At God's command, Isaiah married a prophetess and gave their child the name God chose, as a way of silently speaking to Israel. In obedience to God, Jeremiah remained single; Ezekiel was made a mute except when God chose to speak through him; and Hosea married a very wanton woman. All of this proved to be powerful reinforcements to what God was saying at those particular times.

Preachers are expected to so strongly believe what they are saying that they will practice what they preach. If we don't believe the message enough to obey it, who will? The old adage is still applicable: "Your life speaks so loudly I can't hear what you say."

The Preparation of the Preacher

Preaching is far more than talking about things spiritual. Preaching is communication. It is a skill that demands preparation. Solomon described the wise preacher as "weighing and studying and arranging proverbs with great care" (Ecclesiastes 12:9 RSV). Extemporaneous speaking may sometimes be necessary, but it certainly should be the exception and not the rule. I was startled to hear Charles Swindol say in a radio broadcast, "The greatest crime committed in America today is what is given to congregations over the pulpit Sunday mornings." It is likely that in God's sight that is an accurate statement. So much of what is called preaching today lacks sound preparation, and often it is little more than a restating of old religious platitudes.

Unpreparedness is not spiritual, as some have suggested; it is criminal. God's Spirit is not hindered by preparedness, but He is greatly hampered when He must try to communicate through a person who is not ready. As vital and wonderful as revelation and inspiration are, they cannot substitute for true preparation. The preacher's heart, head, and message all need to be made ready in advance, for " 'out of the abundance of the heart the mouth speaks' " (Matthew 12:34). To produce this abundance, every sincere preacher must learn to dedicate time for praying, reading, studying and preparing sermons. Furthermore, he needs to budget funds for purchasing books and for attending conferences. No one in heaven or on earth can prepare the preacher for his ministry. He must prepare himself with the help of God and men.

Solomon also suggested that "the Preacher sought to find acceptable words" (Ecclesiastes 12:10). Words are the main tools of the preacher, and he needs to know how to use them well, not as a man-pleaser, but as a good communicator. Sometimes the message that God gives is unpalatable, but it does not need to be expressed harshly or unpleasantly. Telling a person that his face would stop a clock will get a far different reaction than telling him that his face is timeless. Basically the message is the same, but the second way of saying it contains a tone of grace and mercy.

Preachers must learn to communicate with people rather than merely talk to people. We all need to avoid religious jargon and sidestep overworked cliches. We must also learn to avoid generalities and be specific. The theological vocabulary of the books we read will likely be strange and meaningless to most of our listeners, so we need to use the vocabulary of the people to whom we are speaking. Jesus was a master of this art. When He was with fishermen, He spoke of fishing, and when He was in the company of farmers, He talked about farming. He seemed to be as comfortable with the vocabulary of women as He was with the speech of tradesmen, and because of this He communicated with people. This is an art we can all learn if we will apply ourselves to it.

Because the preacher constantly deals with an unseen product, he is dependent upon words to make that product desirable. A good dictionary and a thesaurus should never be out of his reach, for the very style or form of speech with which a truth is delivered will deeply affect its reception. Every preacher needs to constantly enlarge his vocabulary and to practice using active verbs and proper nouns. It is one thing to simply say, "We have a tree in our yard," but what a fuller word picture could be painted by saying, "The aromatic Douglas fir towers majestically over our front yard." Dare to be expressive with words.

"The preacher sought to find acceptable words,"

Solomon said, "and what was written was upright —
words of truth" (Ecclesiastes 12:10). The preacher who
desires to improve his communication skills would do
well to do some writing, for it will teach conciseness,
force accuracy, demand structure, and enlarge vocabulary. Writing may well be more perspiration than
inspiration, but its rewards are well worth all the
effort. Beyond the discipline writing produces, its
results will probably reach more people with the
message of Christ than vocal preaching ever would;
furthermore, writing gives a permanence to truth that
speaking cannot give. Jerim, a wise preacher of a past
generation, well stated, "Speaking is but like a burning
coal, which giveth heat and some light near at hand;
but writing is like a shining lamp, which giveth light
afar off."

The Preaching of the Preacher

Solomon also observed, "The Preacher ... still taught
the people knowledge" (Ecclesiastes 12:9). This is the
purpose for all the preparation the preacher has made:
he wants to teach what he has been taught. He yearns
to proclaim the Person of Jesus and the provision of
God in such a way as to make them desirable to his
listeners. Regardless of the format he may use, his goal
is to teach the people the way of the Lord more
perfectly.

The wisest among us cannot communicate his
wisdom by some sudden influence. Even God said that
He would speak to His people, " 'precept upon precept,
precept upon precept, line upon line, line upon line,
here a little, there a little' " (Isaiah 28:13). Good
preachers learn to build truth upon truth using repe-
tition and review as tools of instruction.

Solomon added, "The sayings of the wise are like
goads and like nails firmly fixed" (Ecclesiastes 12:11
RSV). Good preaching will both motivate people into

action like a goad encourages an ox to move forward and will establish those people in the faith as though they had been fastened into God by clinched nails. Good preaching from a prepared preacher will cause people to be "steadfast, immovable, always abounding in the work of the Lord" (1 Corinthians 15:58) and "built together for a habitation of God in the Spirit" (Ephesians 2:22).

We realize, of course, that human preparation and skill will not, in itself, meet the deep needs in the lives of the people to whom we preach. We need a message that is Divine, a manifestation that is spiritual, and a demonstration that only God can supply. Paul confessed, "My speech and my preaching were not with persuasive words of human wisdom, but in demonstration of the Spirit and of power, that your faith should not be in the wisdom of men but in the power of God" (1 Corinthians 2:4).

God delights in giving His preachers a fresh, relevant message, and then He enjoys confirming that word with signs and wonders. Powerful preaching is filled with the power of the Holy Spirit.

Years ago, the English clergyman who was the instructor for the homiletics course in a Bible college repeatedly said, "Gentlemen, prepare as though there were no God, and then preach as though there was no preparation." It was sound advice. We dare not substitute the anointing of the Holy Spirit for advanced preparation, nor should we exchange good preparation for a Divine anointing. The two should go together like a hand in a glove. God has chosen to work through persons, and each person is extremely dependent upon God for every aspect of the preaching ministry. This mutual dependence makes us partners in proclaiming the gospel.

Jesus said that a tree will reproduce fruit according to its nature, and applied this to the Pharisees, saying,

"For out of the abundance of the heart the mouth speaks. A good man out of his heart brings forth good things, and an evil man out of the evil treasure brings forth evil things ... For by your words you will be justified, and by your words you will be condemned" (Matthew 12:34, 35, 37). Obviously, then, preachers will be forced to eat what they serve. If they do it now, it will temper what they say. If they wait until later, it may become the basis for their judgment.

Prayer:

Oh, Lord, it is almost beyond my comprehension that you would choose me to be a preacher of Your Divine truths, but You did! Please keep me from trying to become the message and constantly remind me that I am only the messenger. Draw me regularly into Your presence where I may hear Your voice and sense the feeling of Your heart. Please make me an honest partaker of the things that I proclaim, and deliver me from a feeling of superiority over the people to whom I preach. Amen!"

Chapter 9

Leaders as Partners

"We [are] workers together with Him"
(2 Corinthians 6:1)

After dwelling on the reconciling ministry of God through Jesus Christ, Paul said, "Therefore we are ambassadors for Christ, as though God were pleading through us ...." (2 Corinthians 5:20). From that comes the clear message that none of us works alone. If we are ambassadors, we are on a mission for the government we represent. The words an ambassador speaks express the policy and attitude of his government, and his lifestyle is representative of the country that sent him. In other countries, an American ambassador is viewed as "Mr. United States," but he, better than anyone else, knows that he is only an appointed representative of a great nation.

Jesus said that even the Holy Spirit " 'will not speak on His own authority, but whatever He hears He will speak; and He will tell you things to come. He will glorify Me, for He will take of what is Mine and declare

it to you. All things that the Father has are Mine.
Therefore I said that He will take of Mine and declare it
to you' '' (John 16: 13-15). If indeed the very Spirit of
God works in such a partnership with the Son that He
is restricted from saying anything other than what He
has been advised to say, then surely we who minister
the grace and goodness of God on this earth must be
under even stricter controls. We cannot function independently of God at any time in any matter and still
fulfill our role as heavenly ambassador.

Happy is the Christian minister who has accepted
his role as a representative of God's kingdom. He has
nothing to say until he receives instructions to speak
for heaven. He has nothing to do except what his
heavenly supervisor has declared should be done. He
lives not to please himself, but to represent God on
earth. He is, indeed, a "worker together with God" (*see*
1 Corinthians 2:6).

The Concept of Partnership

Many persons never progress to being partners with
God. Upon meeting Jesus, they quickly become followers of the Lamb, as were the multitudes on the shores of
Galilee during the days of Jesus, and they marvel at
His teaching and revel in His provisions and compassion, but they ever remain spectators or recipients
of His grace. These never become producers; they
remain consumers forever.

Others, as the chosen disciples, receive a limited
empowering and go forth ministering for God. They
delight in being in Divine service, but they maintain an
employer/employee relationship. They minister out of
obedience to a command and are often very legalistic in
the exercise of their ministry. Because they see themselves as employed to serve people, they often become
very need-oriented. Unfortunately, however, those

who become unduly need-regulated soon become need-controlled. Those who merely minister for God often find themselves severely overworked, not because God is a harsh employer, but because there will never be an end to people's needs.

Before His death, Jesus turned to His disciples, who had originally been but followers, and said, " 'No longer do I call you servants, for a servant does not know what his master is doing; but I have called you friends, for all things that I heard from My Father I have made known to you' " (John 15:15). At that moment Jesus invited His maturing disciples into a limited partnership with Himself wherein they would have a voice in management and understand the family business rather than remain as workers who only comprehend their individual tasks. They were promoted from the rank of employee to the position of co-laborers with Christ.

This is Christ's desire for all who enter into spiritual ministry. He prayed to His Father, " 'As You sent Me into the world, I also have sent them into the world' " (John 17:18), and just three verses later he told the Father that He desired " 'that they also may be one in Us' " (John 17:21). Jesus and the Father never lost Their relationship while the earthly ministry was being performed. They were always one — even at Calvary, for Paul wrote that "God was in Christ reconciling the world to Himself" (2 Corinthians 5:19). The redemptive work of Jesus was a partnership between Himself and the Father from conception through completion. Similarly, Jesus says He has sent us into the world as partners with God, implementing the Divine plan as fellow laborers with God. We have already seen that the final book of the Bible depicts this relationship as offices — Jesus has, " 'made us kings [co-regents] and priests to our God; and we shall reign on the earth' " (Revelation 5:10). We reign with and under God. It is His kingdom, but we share its rule with

Him here on the earth. As glorious and unbelievable as it may seem, ministers have been invited into the administration of God's business as partners with God Himself.

Our Conduct as Partners

We are "God's fellow workers" (1 Corinthians 3:9), or, as Williams translated it, "We belong to God as His fellow-workers." This may be voluntary or involuntary, for whether we admit it or not, all persons belong to God, and all will be used by Him as He chooses to use them.

Before my birth, John Oman wrote in *The Paradox of the World*, "All of us alike are God's instruments. By not setting our hearts on wickedness or doing evil with both our hands can we prevent God from using us. Our folly will serve Him, when our wisdom fails; our wrath praises Him, though our wills rebel. Yet, as God's instruments without intention and in our own despite, we generally serve God's ends only as we defeat our own. To be God's agent is quite another matter. This we are only as we learn God's will, respond to His call, work faithfully together with Him, and find our own highest ends in fulfilling His."

The question facing every person, then, is not whether he will be used by God, but whether he will be God's unconscious tool or God's conscious partner. It could be said that all creative or redemptive work is a partnership with God, but it reaches its highest point and deepest satisfaction when we become conscious of union with God, when our work or service becomes an active partnership with Him. All ministers should remind themselves regularly that they are junior partners with God. It is not their business, but His; therefore it is never my ministry, but His ministry. Any ministry we may possess is God-given and should remain God-controlled. It is to be implemented in cooperation with, not in independence from, Him. God is totally independent of us, except as He has chosen to allow us into His work program, but we can never be totally independent of God.

Ours is a very limited partnership, and we are extremely dependent upon our Senior Partner for daily directions, appropriate authority, and reasonable resources. All too frequently, as we become comfortable in the exercise of a spiritual enabling, we tend to see it as our ministry, and we try to operate it from the memory circuits of our carnal minds. Essentially, we have withdrawn from the Divine partnership and have established our own independent business, but we lack the ethics to change the name of the firm, for we desire the prestige and authority that God's name gives to our business.

Such independent action is as foolhardy as the youth director of a large church who tries to start his own church after serving under the senior pastor for less than a year. His success on a limited scale gave him visions of grandeur, but he failed to take into consideration that the facilities he had used, the finances he needed, and the very people to whom he had ministered were all supplied by his senior pastor. His desire for independence destroyed what ministry he had been entrusted with, for his violation of trust made him totally unacceptable as a staff member to any pastor, and his "new church" was aborted before it was fully formed. He rejected a working partnership, but he was too immature to function independently.

So are all of us who give ourselves to ministry. As a working member of God's team we function well in our little sphere of trust, but whenever pride causes us to seek to "set out on our own," we are doomed from the very beginning. Paul had to write rather harshly to the Galatians, saying, "O foolish Galatians! Who has bewitched you that you should not obey the truth ...

Are you so foolish? Having begun in the Spirit, are you now being made perfect by the flesh?'' (Galatians 3:1, 3).

One of the first principles to be learned in a partnership is that there can be no unilateral decisions. A happy marriage calls for bilateral choices, and a successful business partnership demands the voice of all partners in major decisions. We who have entered into ministerial partnerships with God must learn that while God gives us a voice in the operation of our ministry, that voice is not exclusive. God's will always overrides our will.

Jesus beautifully demonstrated this relationship, for He consistently told His disciples that everything He did was an extension of the Father. He spoke what the Father said, He submitted His will at all times to the will of the Father, He exercised the judgment given to Him by the Father, and even testified, " 'The Son can do nothing of Himself, but what He sees the Father do; for whatever He does, the Son also does in like manner' '' (John 5:19).

This is our pattern for working in partnership with God. No matter how great we may become in the exercise of "our" ministries, we can never override God. Even a large convention of ministers cannot outvote God. If God said it, that settles it, and we might just as well get involved in doing it. The veto power is invested in the Senior Partner, not in the junior members of the firm.

The very positive facet of this partnership with God is that the responsibility for the plan rests with God. Our responsibility is only to implement that revealed plan. As Paul illustrated it, we but plant the seed and water it; God gives the increase (*see* 1 Corinthians 3:7). The key to successful ministry, then, is not working, but co-working with God. When we have done our part, we can look to God to accomplish His. Knowing that we are partners with God is the secret of inexhaustible strength, for we have access to all of heaven's resources — mental, physical, and spiritual. "I can do all things through Christ who strengthens me," Paul testified (Philippians 4:13).

Our Companionship as Partners

God refuses to consider Himself a silent partner. He does not fund the operation for a percentage of the profits and remain uninvolved in the operation of the business. It is His business, and we have become partners not because of what we can contribute to the firm, but because of Divine grace. Like the parent who involves the children in household chores both for instruction and for fellowship of doing, we have been invited into the family firm more for companionship than for our competence. In being invited to set His table, we enjoy a measure of companionship with God, especially if we will do it *with* Him rather than *for* Him.

To many ministers, receiving work instructions is the extent of verbal companionship with God, so He insures our return to His presence in the near future by giving us insufficient instructions to start with. If, however, we accept partial plans as though they were definitive demands, we will not only fail in our mission but will frustrate God's desire for more relationship time with us. Just as discussing the vacation plans often proves to be more valuable to a marriage than the actual vacation, talking over the program with God is often more important to Him than its implementation. God loves to talk with His partners, and He will regularly call us into fellowship. Paul said it well: "God is faithful, by whom you were called into the fellowship of His Son, Jesus Christ our Lord" (1 Corinthians 1:9).

If there was ever a disciple who knew fellowship with the Lord, it was the Apostle John, but it is he who spoke of a horizontal fellowship as well as a vertical one. He wrote, "That which we have seen and heard we declare to you, that you also may have fellowship with us; and truly our fellowship is with the Father and with His Son Jesus Christ" (1 John 1:3). Christian ministers are fellow-laborers both with God and with one another. We are in the same business, members of the same firm, and partners with the same Senior Partner.

When Paul learned that the Corinthians were dividing themselves over the Divine channel that was used to bring them into God's grace, he wrote, "Who then is Paul, and who is Apollos, but ministers through whom you believed, as the Lord gave to each one? I planted, Apollos watered, but God gave the increase" (1 Corinthians 3:5, 6). They were not only in cooperation with God in this harvest, they were co-laborers together in God's business to produce this harvest.

In the ministries that God has placed in His body, there is a difference in natural powers, in spiritual gifts, in ecclesiastical position, and even in length of service, but each is needed for his specific task. God who employs each of them is the One Who is ultimately responsible for the garden and for all work that is done in His earthly Eden. Our responsibility ends when we have done what we were instructed to do harmoniously with what others have already done.

How careful key leaders in the ministry must be lest they project that "their" ministry is the only important one. It is only important if that is what is needed at the time. Few things are less important than a plow during harvest season or the combine during the irrigating period. There is a time and a place for all ministries in the body of Christ, but leadership must make room for these ministries.

Paul never thought of himself as a solo act. He wrote, "If anyone inquires about Titus, he is my partner and fellow worker concerning you" (Titus 8:23). He worked with Barnabas, Silas, John Mark, Timothy, and many others, and although he remained the Apostle among them, he made room for their ministries and joyfully gave credit for their contributions.

As marvelous as the ministry from the pulpit may be, it should never supplant the ministry from the pew. God doesn't say and do everything through one person, and Mister "Hoe" and Sister "Shovel" are often the most practical tools for the task at hand. True ministers quickly recognize true ministries and make room for their operation, knowing that God, the Senior Partner in this farming business, has called a great variety of workmen and has gifted them in specialties that will make the crop all the more productive.

However, God has no "silent partners"; all of us are actively engaged in His ministry. We do not sit in an office, giving orders to others — we stand side by side with God and His workmen in whatever labor is to be done. However, we increasingly see Christian leaders declare a partnership with a fellowship or a denomination, but when that group disagrees with actions or attitudes, these leaders withdraw from that fellowship rather than accept reprimand or discipline. It is exciting to realize that we are partners with God, but it is necessary to truly honor the partnership God has given us one with another. If we preach it, we should practice it. Partners, too, should eat what they serve.

Prayer:

Dear Jesus, how can I ever thank You enough for promoting me from a servant of God to be a partner with You? I never dreamed when You called me into Your service that I would be working alongside You. Your presence destroys all sense of labor, and I find myself rejoicing all day long that although we are infinitely different, You are making me useful unto Yourself. Please help me to relate lovingly to the other partners with whom You have called me to work, for some of them are very difficult to associate with. I pray this in Jesus' lovely name. Amen!

Chapter 10

Leaders as Patterns

"You have us for a pattern" (Philippians 3:17)

When God prepared to repopulate His renovated earth, He said, " 'Let Us make man in Our image, according to Our likeness' "(Genesis 1:26). God used Himself as the pattern for man. Much later, when God instructed Moses to build the Tabernacle in the wilderness, He repeatedly said, " 'See that you make all things according to the pattern shown you on the mountain' " (Hebrews 8:5; *see* Exodus 25:9, 40; Numbers 8:4). God builds according to a pattern, and when He involves man in that construction He insists that a pattern be followed exactly.

In God's economy, everything follows a format. All of nature reproduces itself according to a genetic pattern; all robins look alike, and sparrows throughout the world resemble each other and have the same habit patterns. Even races of people have very similar characteristics both physically and emotionally. There is, of course, allowance for individuality, but God's creativity follows a prescribed pattern. All long-needle pine trees are basically the same, though the placement of the limbs varies greatly. Perhaps the greatest differences in life are to be seen in people, but even there the similarities are far greater than the differences.

The development of science has been possible because of the unchangeable laws of nature, which indicate that everything functions according to a pattern. Pure water consistently freezes at thirty-two degrees Fahrenheit, and light always travels at the speed of 186,000 miles per second. God created all things according to a pattern.

Even in the spiritual realm, God works according to a pattern. Take, for example, the law of faith or the law of giving. They are not laws in the sense of being statutes or commands, but they are principles that work as inexorably as the laws of gravity or refraction. They are patterns that, if followed, will produce a predetermined effect. God's goal of bringing us back into His image will be achieved not through caprice but through conformity to a pattern. God is restoring us bit by bit, but He knows from the beginning how each piece will fit into the whole structure.

Jesus Christ is, of course, the Master Pattern for all of our lives, but a project as massive as transforming sinful men into the Divine image requires that this pattern be broken into smaller segments, just as a dress pattern has many pieces that must be laid out on the material individually and cut before being sewn together. This is where God's ministers come into the program. God has chosen to form His ministers into segments of the pattern of the Divine image, and He uses these parts to shape others to fit into His scheme of reconstruction. Paul told the Philippians, "The things which you learned and received and heard and saw in me, these do, and the God of peace will be with you"(Philippians 4:9).

Leaders Are Visualizations of Christ

All patterns work from the concept of the finished product down to the individual components that will make that product possible. The architect first sketches his projection of the exterior elevations of the building. Then he draws details of the foundation, the wall construction and the roof structure. Similarly, God likes to show a drawing of the finished product by etching it upon the lives of His ministers. When others can see Christ in and through us, they have some concept of what God has chosen to make them become.

Frankly, people must see before they will submit to change. Many years ago, the congregation I was pastoring desperately needed new facilities, but no amount of talking could unite us on a plan. However, when I took time to make a scale model of the structure I saw as viable for us, and allowed the congregation to view, touch, and discuss it, a unanimous vote to build was reached in the first meeting. The people merely needed help to visualize the completed product before they would commit their time, energies, and monies to the plan. In like manner, God has chosen to make His ministers scale models or photos of the finished product so people can form a concept of what they can become by committing themselves to the dealings of God in their lives. In a very real sense, ministers are a reproduction of the front elevation of the master plan that God has drawn. The New Testament declares, "For it is the God who commanded light to shine out of darkness who has shone in our hearts to give the light of the knowledge of the glory of God in the face of Jesus Christ" (2 Corinthians 4:6). All who have ever worked in a photographic darkroom recognize this imagery. God is the light, Christ is the negative, and we are the sensitized paper. God shines upon us through Christ Jesus, and when we are properly processed we bear the image of God's dear Son, Who is God's demonstration of the finished product.

Shortly before making this statement, Paul had said, "But we all, with unveiled face, beholding as in a mirror the glory of the Lord, are being transformed into the same image from glory to glory, just as by the Spirit of the Lord" (2 Corinthians 3:18). It speaks to the same illustration, for what is focused upon us — the glory of the Lord — is what we become. The photographic paper "beholding" the bright image of the negative takes on the positive image in permanent form.

All Christians should bear the image of God, but it is imperative that God's leaders become a visualization of Christ, for we "have put on the new man who is renewed in knowledge according to the image of Him who created him" (Colossians 3:10), and "As we have borne the image of the man of dust, we shall also bear the image of the heavenly Man" (1 Corinthians 15:49). Where will the people look to see Christ if not to the minister?

Many years ago, God brought into my life a minister who so demonstrated Christ that I determined to have what he had at all costs. It was almost like the "before" and "after" photos often used in advertising. I was the "before"; he was the "after." I saw what I could become by seeing a picture of Christ in him. Without this image, I would never have given myself to the working of the Holy Spirit to effect the necessary radical changes in me.

This is a consistent principle, for God is working not on inanimate material but on persons who have wills that must surrender to God's intervention in their lives. Until they see what they can become, they will not allow their lives to be completely rearranged by God's Spirit within them.

How imperative it is that we be a true engraving or

an undistorted picture of Christ, for unless we look like Jesus, people will have a distorted image of Him. What people see in our lives as ministers affects them far more than what they hear us say. Paul counseled Titus, "In all things showing yourself to be a pattern of good works; in doctrine showing integrity, reverence, incorruptibility, sound speech that cannot be condemned, that one who is an opponent may be ashamed, having nothing evil to say of you" (Titus 2:7, 8).

We are far more than proclaimers of Christ; we are pictures of Jesus. We are the front elevation of the master plan. We are the pictured meal in the book of recipes. We depict the finished product in visual form, and God uses us as an enticement to draw others into the process of change.

Leaders Are Templates of Christ

All who have been involved with construction, whether a hobby project or a commercial enterprise, are familiar with a template. It is a piece of wood or metal that has the exact form, shape, and size of the piece to be cut from the construction material. When the roof of the house is being built, the carpenter will lay out the first rafter with his tape measure and square, determining its length, angle of top and bottom cuts, and the notch that allows the rafter to sit on the top plate of the wall. When this first rafter is cut, it becomes the template for cutting all subsequent rafters. This is a time-saving device.

Similarly, Christ first forms His ministers and then uses them as models for shaping others who will be used in the building of God's holy temple. The New Testament tells us that "whom He foreknew, He also predestined to be conformed to the image of His Son, that He might be the firstborn among many brethren" (Romans 8:29). Christ is, of course, the complete Pattern, but He has made His ministers templates of individual segments of the full plan. We are preshaped for what-ever portion of the building we have been formed to fit. Since God does not need all rafters, He does not shape all His ministers into rafter templates. Some will be templates for the wall studs, while others may be shaped into floor joists, but each of us is formed into a template to reproduce the image that God has made us to become.

Paul dared to write, "Brethren, join in following my example, and note those who so walk, as you have us for a pattern" (Philippians 3:17), and "Hold fast the pattern of sound words which you have heard from me, in faith and love which are in Christ Jesus" (2 Timothy 1:13). Paul knew that he was a preformed template of God's design and that what God had done in him should be transferred to the lives of others. He even went so far as to say, "Therefore I urge you, imitate me" (1 Corinthians 4:16).

Almost in spite of our preaching, people will become what we are rather than what we proclaim. Some years ago, I frequently ministered in a church with a compassionate pastor whose preaching was weak and whose doctrine was immature and sometimes very marginal to the truth, but he had gathered around him a group of saints who had become loving and compassionate persons reaching out to the distressed and oppressed with the tenderness of Jesus. They had become what he was because God had used him as a template in forming their lives. His life, not his lips, had changed them.

The men God used in the Bible were more patterns than proclaimers, for ministry is more a lifestyle than it is a profession. Daniel's way of living was his ministry in Babylon, and, as ministers of the grace of God, so will ours be. Jesus said in His Sermon on the Mount, " 'Let your light so shine before men, that they may see your good works and glorify your Father in heaven' '' (Matthew 5:16).

Leaders Are Vehicles for the Formation of Others

When Paul wrote that "[God] also made us sufficient as ministers of the new covenant, not of the letter but of the Spirit; for the letter kills, but the Spirit gives life" (2 Corinthians 3:6), he made God responsible not only for our commission, but for our competency to fulfill that commission. God, Who chooses where we will fit in His ministerial program, also forms us into the exact pattern He needs. Sometimes, as we have seen, He forms us into a template so that others are made into our very image, but other times He makes us into a form, a mold, or a die that will be the mirror image of what the final product will bear. There seems to be at least an allusion to this in Paul's insistence that our ministry is "not of the letter but of the Spirit," although we know that the product of true ministry is to bring people's lives into harmony with the written Word of God.

There are times when we ministers are the form into which human concrete is poured, thus determining the permanent shape of the product. Through the years, I have noticed that teaching pastors generally produce teachers in their congregations, while those with evangelistic ministries form other evangelists, and materialistically minded ministers tend to produce self-centered humanists as their followers. In the natural world, concrete is basically the same in walks, steps, foundations, and dams, but the form into which it is poured determines what it becomes. Similarly, the pliable redeemed life is all the same substance; its use comes from the shape of the form into which it is poured. Ministers are the mold into which God has hand-carved His image, intending to cast the lives of others in us so that they too may bear the image of the Divine.

During the 100th anniversary renovation of the Statue of Liberty, the world's tallest free-form scaffolding was erected around the grand old lady to enable workmen to make latex molds of this mammoth structure. From these molds were made castings which, in turn, were used to form replacement parts that were exactly like the original. One hundred years from now these same molds can be used to cast replacement parts that will fit the structure perfectly, for they were formed on the original.

The Bible speaks of Jesus "being the brightness of His [God's] glory and the express image of His person" (Hebrews 1:3). We could say that Jesus brought to us the latex mold of God, and God loves to cast His ministers into this mold to form a reverse image that can be used for the forming of that Divine image in others. Perhaps this is why Paul could confidently say, "Imitate me, just as I also imitate Christ" (1 Corinthians 11:1). Paul had no desire to turn out "miniature Pauls," but he had a passion to see Christ formed into the lives of others, and he was willing to be God's mold into which those lives were poured.

Not all metal is formed by pouring. Many manufacturers use a process called stamping, in which dies are formed in a mirror image of the desired finished product and sheet metal is pressed onto these dies with extreme pressure. In a very real sense, ministers are formed into God's dies and are used to stamp the image of God into the hearts of believers. All who have given themselves to the work of the ministry can relate to the tremendous pressure that sometimes accompanies the exercise of their ministries. The human heart does not yield easily, and lives will not change without great outside pressure, so God uses His ministers to exert this life-changing pressure as raw material is stamped into usable parts.

Of course, no casting or stamping emerges from the process ready to be used. It will need trimming, polishing, and correcting of imperfections, but the shape and form have been established; the heavy work has been accomplished. Long after the minister has allowed God to use him in forming others, there will be the inner working of the Holy Spirit in these lives to make them more and more like Jesus, but the rough work is quickly done through the lives of God's special servants.

In all three figures — the form, the mold, the die — we deal with a mirror image, or the reverse of the desired finished product. As incredible as it may seem, God often chooses to do in the life of His chosen minister the exact opposite of what He intends to do *through* him. Corrie ten Boom knew years of suffering, cruelty, and slavery in Nazi prison camps, but it formed her into an image of a healing, loving, emancipating God, and thousands of lives have been stamped with this reverse image by coming into contact with her.

Paul was aware of this great contrast between the ministering Apostles and the Corinthian believers, for he wrote, "We are fools for Christ's sake, but you are wise in Christ! We are weak, but you are strong! You are distinguished, but we are dishonored! Being reviled, we bless; being persecuted, we endure it; being defamed, we entreat" (1 Corinthians 4:10, 12, 13) and then added, "Therefore I urge you, imitate me" (verse 16). Paul did not want them to suffer what he suffered, but he wanted them to become the image of Christ that had been etched in his life. He was willing to undergo anything necessary to become an accurate die or mold that could stamp or form the image of Christ into the Gentile believers. So must we!

Ministers of all categories must be willing to bear the

impression of the Divine in their human nature so that others may be molded, formed, or stamped into the Divine image. What we are is what they will become, so we must be accurate in all details. We must meticulously picture Christ, for all imperfections in us will be reproduced in those to whom we minister. We must eat what we serve!

Prayer:

Lord, I thank You for the pattern my earthly father and other godly men set before my young life. Thank you for helping me to see Jesus in them. Now, Lord Jesus, I am the pattern to which others look. Please help me to reveal You in Your strength and glory. Let me be a godly example in my life as well as in my ministry, for others are forming their lives in the mold of my ministry. Without Your help, I could ruin them for time and eternity. Sometimes this responsibility seems more than I am able to bear, but if You form me into the pattern of Your will, then others, in conforming to the pattern of my life, will also find themselves in God's perfect will. Thank You for accepting the responsibility for this. In Jesus' name. Amen!

Chapter 11

Leaders as Pierced Ones

"My ears you have pierced" (Psalm 40:6, NIV)

If ever there was a nation that fully understood the evils and suffering of slavery, it was Israel. During the more than three hundred years they served as slaves to Egypt, their bondage had grown increasingly severe until God sovereignly delivered them and led them into the wilderness to teach them how to live as free persons. At the beginning of this educational process, God gave the people the law, commandments, statutes, and judgments on Mount Sinai as guidelines for behavior in all of life's situations. Among these written codes were specific rules for the treatment of slaves and servants, for God well knew that freedom from tyranny often makes tyrants of the freed persons as they inflict revengefully upon others what was previously imposed upon them.

Historic record demonstrates that the oppressed often become the oppressors — even in religious circles. God, Who understands our character better than we understand ourselves, knew that the potential for over-reaction was great among these recently freed Hebrews, so He made legal provision to protect those who would become bond-men to these Hebrews.

The Provision for Servants

The slaves who served these Hebrews when they got into the land were acquired through subsequent warfare, for qualified workers were considered a choice spoil of war. They could be bought, sold, given away, or released, and their children automatically became the chattel property of their master.

These were slaves in every sense of the word, but in the Law God made provisions to help prevent their complete dehumanization. They were guaranteed a sabbath rest (*see* Exodus 20:10); they could share in the religious feasts (*see* Deuteronomy 12:12, 18); they were provided refuge if they fled from their masters (*see* Deuteronomy 23:15, 16); and they were given freedom if they were maimed by their masters.

Of course, there were occasions when a Hebrew served another Hebrew, but they were called servants rather than slaves. They usually came into this indentured service through mishandled debt (*see* 2 Kings 4:1) or as punishment for theft (*see* Exodus 22:2, 3). They had all the protection afforded slaves plus much more, for God said, " 'If one of your brethren who dwells by you becomes poor, and sells himself to you, you shall not compel him to serve as a slave. But as a hired servant and a sojourner he shall be with you ...' " (Leviticus 25:39-40).

It is a mistake for us to interpret these protective regulations of the Law as God's establishing or even sanctioning slavery, for God's Word consistently reaches persons where they are and gradually lifts them to higher standards of living. God merely recognized slavery as normative for a society that had known nothing else for longer than the United States has been a nation. Abolition of slavery at that time would have been incomprehensible to these Hebrews, so God simply made provision to protect the rights and personal dignity of the slaves and servants in Israel. It is likely that this "Bill of Rights" for slaves seemed ultraliberal to the Hebrews. In subsequent years, God had to speak quite harshly through His prophets to the land-holders who would not grant slaves and servants their rights.

Just as Egypt found it impossible to maintain its economy without the slave work force, so the Hebrews found the many demands of agrarian life more than they could meet without manpower. Since God had given a farm to each family and had prohibited the transfer of that land to anyone other than a direct descendant, workers were in short supply. The farmers could occasionally hire a workman, but they far preferred to purchase a slave or a "servant," as the Hebrew bondman was called. (By the way, that is exactly what persons who are worshippers of God and workers with God are called: "servants." This title has been given to kings, priests, prophets, and handmaidens. It is the Bible's favorite title for Moses, and it is used often for the followers of Christ. We are not merely workers — we are servants. We who were once slaves to sin have now become "servants of Christ, doing the will of God from the heart, with good will doing service, as to the Lord, and not to men" according to Ephesians 6:6-7.)

How easily we who are ministers unto the Lord forget that we are not the masters of the people — we are servants of our heavenly Master, and at His bidding we serve His children. Whether that service is extended in leadership as a king, in instruction as a teaching priest, in communicating a message from the Father as a prophet, or merely in washing the feet of the heirs of God, it is the ministry of a servant. All true ministers have been captured by the overwhelming love of God as displayed at Calvary; and, as Paul reminded us, we "were bought at a price; therefore glorify God in your body and in your spirit, which are God's" (1 Corinthians 6:20).

In our democratic society with its current emphasis upon humanism, the very idea of being a servant to another is distasteful, and even in our religious circles the quest for greatness and recognition often supplants the ministry of serving. Still, Jesus is spoken of as God's servant four times in the book of Acts alone (*see* Acts 3:13, 26; 4:27, 30), and Paul said that Jesus "made Himself of no reputation, taking the form of a servant" (Philippians 2:7). This Servant, Jesus, taught His disciples, " 'a servant is not greater than his master' " (John 13:16; 15:20). If Jesus was the servant of the One Who sent Him, how dare we think of ourselves as anything higher than a servant?

The whole concept of ministry is service, whether that ministry flows out of an office, through the gifts of the Spirit, by compassion, or even in merely sharing hospitality. Ministry is a need-meeting service that may or may not be reciprocal. Jesus testified, " 'Even the Son of Man did not come to be served, but to serve, and to give His life a ransom for many' " (Mark 10:45). The person who enters the professional ministry expecting to have people serve him and meet his needs is in the wrong field of endeavor, for being a servant involves giving and doing, not getting and having done for you. "Jesus called [the disciples] to Himself and said to them, 'You know that those who are considered rulers over the Gentiles lord it over them, and their great ones exercise authority over them. Yet it shall not be so among you; but whoever desires to become great among you shall be your servant. And whoever of you desires to be first shall be slave of all' " (Mark 10:42-44).

The Position of a Servant

The Hebrew servant was not treated as a slave, and the variety of tasks that were entrusted to him ranged from field or house work to management of the business affairs of the master. Servants were often given great authority, even carrying the seal that represented the signature of their master and actually conducting business in his name. Many servants were treated as members of the family.

Even a casual student of the Word will recognize that this is exactly what Christ meant when He spoke of us doing Kingdom business "in His name." We, His entrusted servants, carry the seal of the Spirit and have Divine authority in the spirit world, not because of our offices or ministries, but because we function as authorized servants of Jesus Christ who are accepted members "of the household of faith" (Galatians 6:10).

All the personal needs of the Hebrew servant were provided by his master. Housing, clothing, food, and transportation were benefits that went with the position. Frequently, the master even provided a wife for a single servant. In many ways, the position afforded more security than the servants had ever known as free persons.

Knowing this, Paul could confidently assure the servants of the Lord, "My God shall supply all your need according to His riches in glory by Christ Jesus" (Philippians 4:19). Those servants of Christ who have learned to abandon themselves in the affairs of God quickly discover that God can provide for their physical, emotional, spiritual, and financial needs far better than they ever were able to do for themselves, for God supplies according to *His* riches, and even His "leftovers" are superior to our best provisions.

One might see a parallel between a Hebrew servant and a U.S. serviceman. Both are under contract for a specific time; each takes orders from a higher authority; each has a chance to be placed according to his ability; each lives off the provision of the one that is served. The contract becomes mutually beneficial. And so it is in serving the Lord. We can be profitable servants, while, in turn, profiting from this relationship.

The Release of Servants

While slaves, acquired from other nations, could be kept for their lifetimes, God mercifully set a limit on the length of time a Hebrew had to serve his master. The Law stated, "If you buy a Hebrew servant, he shall serve six years; and in the seventh he shall go out free and pay nothing. If he comes in by himself, he shall go out by himself; if he comes in married, then his wife shall go out with him" (Exodus 21:2, 3). The Law given to the second generation added, " 'And when you send him away free from you, you shall not let him go away empty-handed; you shall supply him liberally from your flock, from your threshing floor, and from your winepress. From what the LORD has blessed you with, you shall give to him. You shall remember that you were a slave in the land of Egypt, and the LORD your God redeemed you; therefore I command you this thing today' " (Deuteronomy 16:13, 15).

How marvelously this provision kept hope alive in the heart of the indentured Hebrew, for he could see freedom getting closer every year, and that freedom included all the necessary supplies with which to start a new life. No other nation on earth made such a provision for servants, and neither does sin or the world system. Only Jesus Christ offers complete freedom and release for His servants.

Interestingly enough, God also set a time limit upon the service of the Levite priests. They entered Divine service at age thirty and were released from further service at age fifty (*see* Numbers 4:3), so they served twenty years, or about three compulsory terms for a Hebrew servant.

There is good reason to believe that many of the prophets mentioned in the Scriptures served their prophetic office for only a portion of their lives. Perhaps modern Christianity is asking too high a consecration in requesting persons to make lifetime commitments to Christian service. Many missionary organizations are discovering the value of renewable short-term assignments, for far more persons are willing to give three to seven years of their lives to service for God in another country than are willing to make lifetime dedications. Modern transportation and communications have made this a viable option, for today's missionary can reach more persons in seven years than the pioneer missionaries reached in an entire lifetime.

For the Hebrew servant, the beginning of the seventh year meant forgiveness of all outstanding debts, release from compulsory service, and an opportunity to pick up his life where it had been interrupted by his term of servitude. He once again became his own person, totally responsible for his life. Food, clothing, shelter, and employment were no longer automatic for the freed servant; he had to provide everything his family needed. He quickly learned that freedom has both its price and its responsibility.

Is it possible that something similar to this happens to Christian ministers? After being in God's service for six or twelve years, do they accept the Law's provision of release from compulsory service? Paul's statement "Therefore you are not longer a slave but a son, and if a son, then an heir of God through Christ" (Galatians 4:7) which was intended to release us from the control of the Law, may have instead been applied to the control of Christ. But Paul had already declared, "The heir, as long as he is a child, does not differ at all from a slave, although he is master of all" (Galatians 4:1).

Perhaps those who have traded service with the Lord for independence from the Lord feel that they have already achieved full spiritual maturity, but sonship need not invalidate our servitude; it merely enhances our relationship with the One we serve.

There seem to be so many full-time ministers who are doing their own thing that we dare to assume that their freedom meant more to them than did their service to the Master. The words Jesus spoke to His disciples have been appropriated by some ministers as authority to exchange their servitude for friendship, for, after all, Jesus did say, " 'No longer do I call you servants, for a servant does not know what his master is doing; but I have called you friends' "(John 15:15). They fail to recognize that those words followed Jesus' definitive statement "You are my friends if you do whatever I command you" (John 15:14). This friendship is the outgrowth of obedient service, not a replacement of it.

The desire to end compulsory service by exchanging the role of servant for the role of son or friend may be inherent in each of us. Possibly this freedom is available to us after the sixth year of service, but from the moment we exert our freedom we will be working our own farm and accepting full responsibility for our lives and the lives of our family members. It may be delightful to call it "my ministry" and "my church," but the responsibility of such independence from God's service is terrifying. One may argue that such freedom is merely a changed relationship rather than a broken one, but regardless of how it is viewed, the one who once was in the service of the Master is now in his own service, and no matter how friendly the relationship may remain, the loss to the Master is irreversible.

The Law's Provision for Voluntary Servitude

The end of the sixth year of service was a time of decision for the Hebrew servant. Was his freedom worth its price? If he had been given a wife by his master, she remained a servant in that household for her entire life. Could he leave his wife and children just to be independent? Then he had to consider his relationship to his master, as well as the fact that his current friends and acquaintances were in this part of the land, while his property was likely far away. Frequently, the servant achieved both a standard of living and a status far above anything he could hope to achieve on his own, and this had to be weighed against the benefits of going out free. Freedom meant starting life all over again.

Each servant had to make a permanent decision. The Law's provision was, " 'If the servant plainly says, "I love my master, my wife, and my children, I will not go out free," then his master shall bring him to the judges. He shall also bring him to the door, or to the doorpost, and his master shall pierce his ear with an awl; and he shall serve him forever' " (Exodus 21:5-7).

In actual practice, a golden earring was inserted in this pierced ear to keep this symbol of perpetual servitude from closing up and ceasing to be visible. This use of the earring may have been a carry-over from Israel's years in Egyptian slavery, for the Egyptian priests wore golden earrings as both a symbol of their perpetual service to their gods and as a indication of their ability to hear their gods speak. Part of the tragedy of the golden calf incident at the base of Mount Sinai was the fact that the calf was molded exclusively from golden earrings. Israel surrendered her pledge of service and right to hear from God to make an idol, and in doing so exerted an independence from God's service that extended right into the Babylonian captivity hundreds of years later.

I have wondered if it might be valuable to force all professional ministers to make their decision for freedom or perpetual servitude at the end of their first six years of service. By that time, they should fully understand the blessings and the bitterness, the responsibility and the rewards, and the joy and pain of full-time service of the Divine Master and should be qualified to make a lifetime decision to leave that service or to stay in it forever. This would perpetually free them from the indecision and vacillation that plague so many of today's ministers. The kingdom of God would benefit if a minister would get either in or out of Divine service and stop trying to be both in and out, for, " 'No servant can serve two masters' " (Luke 16:13). The minister who tries dual service is "double-minded man, unstable in all his ways" (James 1:8), and the Word says, "I hate the double-minded" (Psalm 119:113).

The admonition is "Draw near to God and He will draw near to you ... purify your hearts, you double-minded" (James 4:8). Perhaps a lifetime decision after six years would permanently purify the heart at least from vacillation in the matter of being a servant.

The Hebrew servant who loved his master, wife, family, and position more than he loved his independence became a love-slave, and his golden earring was a silent message to everyone that he was not for sale. C. F. Keil, the great German theologian of a past generation, observed, "This act was not prescribed in the law as symbolizing anything shameful or despicable .... It was allowed because love and the allegiance of love was prized more highly than loveless personal freedom" (*Biblical Archaeology*).

Paul began his epistle to the saints in Rome by saying, "Paul, a servant of Jesus Christ," and the Greek word he used denoted a "love slave." Paul proclaimed himself one who had voluntarily gone to the doorpost and allowed the Lord to pierce his ear, in effect fastening him to the house forever. Paul's retirement came when they beheaded him in Rome.

Under inspiration David wrote, "Sacrifice and offering you did not desire, but my ears you have pierced; ... To do your will, O my God, is my desire" (Psalm 40:6, 8, NIV). David, too, belonged to the group of "pierced-ear" ministers. He became a love-slave who could never get out of serving the Lord both as a leader of God's people and as a worshipper of God.

When the writer of the book of Hebrews was establishing the complete vicarity of Christ's coming, he quoted this portion of Psalm 40 (*see* Hebrews 10:5-7), thereby identifying Jesus as a love-slave of God. He was not merely pierced symbolically in the ear lobe; He was pierced in His hands, feet, and side. Christ ever remains the servant-Son of God.

The Ramifications of Love-Service

The movement of the earring was a constant reminder to the Hebrew servant that he was not, and never would be, his own, but had forever surrendered himself to his master. Paul tried to communicate this to the church in Corinth, for he wrote, "Do you not know ... you are not your own? For you were bought at a price; therefore glorify God in your body, and in your spirit, which are God's" (1 Corinthians 6:19, 20), and "You were bought at a price; do not become slaves of men" (1 Corinthians 7:23). The earring of the love-slave declared what a woman's wedding ring is supposed to declare — "I'm already taken!"

Pierced-ear people have made a lifetime commitment that makes it profitable for the Lord to invest training, authority, and all necessary tools in them, for none of this will be lost at the end of six years. Love-slaves own nothing except what the Master gives them, but the best gifts are always reserved for the one who is consistently faithful in the Master's service. They do only what they are directed to do, but that direction carries with it the full authority and abilities of the Master. They will never know freedom, but they are guaranteed that the Master can never dispose of them at some later date, for the Law made no provision for the renunciation of this love-slave relationship by either party. The same earring that announced to others that the servant was not for sale also spoke of continual security to the servant.

God has a great sufficiency of six-year servants. He is looking for more pierced-ear servants who have made a lifetime commitment with no greater reward promised than " 'Well done, good and faithful servant; you were faithful over a few things, I will make you ruler over many things. Enter into the joy of your lord' " (Matthew 25:21).

Just before His arrest, He washed the feet of His disciples and then said, "A servant is not greater than his master; nor is he who is sent greater than he who sent him" (John 13:16). We who have entered into a love-slave relationship with God need to remind ourselves that, although we have entered into the security of Divine love, we are still servants. Our calling is to wash feet and to serve our Master's needs. It is improper for us to expect others to serve us. We need to eat what we serve!

Prayer:

Dear Jesus, the very nature of the message You have given me to preach calls for a lifetime commitment to You. Forgive me for expecting more from others than I am willing to do myself. Take me to the doorway of Your presence and pierce my ear, making me Your perpetual love-slave. Put a ring in my ear to let the world, the flesh, and the devil know that I am unavailable to anyone but You, Lord. I surrender all rights to myself, to recognitions for what I do, and to being remunerated for services rendered. Whenever You see my earring, remember, O Lord, that I'm Yours to command! Amen!

Chapter 12

Leaders as Partakers

"Your words were found, and I ate them"
(Jeremiah 15:16)

It has become expected that the promises of a campaigning politician will not be kept, and it is almost as routine that a preacher will not practice what he preaches. "Do as I say, not as I do" is an accepted norm for most ministry in America today, but it was never so in Bible days. God has always required those in His service to be partakers with the people to whom He sent them. Moses ate the same manna that Israel ate, David shared the cave of Adullam with the 400 persons who had submitted to his leadership, Jeremiah lived through the capture of Jerusalem with the very people to whom he had prophesied since his childhood, and Ezekiel was carried into Babylon as one of the captives. God did not isolate these men from the people they served; they were partakers of the provisions, privations, blessings, and banishments God brought upon His chosen nation.

Since God does not change, it is overdue for ministers in America to stop functioning with double standards. We must be what we preach that others should be, or we should go back to "tent making." We must either be willing to eat what we are serving or become willing to serve what we are eating. The day when hypocrisy, the plural standard, and double-dealing are accepted in the ministry is disappearing. We're too close to the end of time to play the games we have played in the past and call that "ministry." We must either become sincere, honest partakers of our ministry, or we're going to be replaced by those who are. If we don't get with it, God will find persons who will, and we'll find ourselves bypassed and without a ministry.

The Pattern Stated

Because all ministry must find its authority in the Word of God, and since all vocal ministry is a sharing of God's wonderful Book, it is obvious that all who minister must first be partakers of the Bible itself. We've already seen that God commanded the kings to make a handwritten copy of the Law and read it daily (*see* Deuteronomy 17:15-20), but the same principle is given for those who ministered in other offices. God's Word to Isaiah was " 'Search from the book of the LORD and read' " (Isaiah 34:16), and Paul told Timothy, "Till I come, give attention to reading" (1 Timothy 4:13). Jeremiah, Ezekiel and John were commanded to eat God's Word (*see* Jeremiah 15:16, Ezekiel 3:1-3, Revelation 10:8-11), and Job declared, "I have treasured the words of His mouth more than my necessary food" (Job 23:12). These men found their sustenance in the very message they were given. God so filled them with His Word that even when they and their messages were rejected they could not change that message, for from the abundance of their hearts, God's Word poured forth.

We, too, need to ingest the Word before we seek to express a vocal ministry, and we desperately need to feast on the Word after ministry both for strength and for something fresh to give to the people. God's message comes not from the mind, but from the innermost being of the messenger, for God chooses to communicate from Spirit to spirit or heart to heart. Reading or hearing is one thing, but digesting and profiting by it is quite another. The psalmist wisely wrote, "I will mediate on Your precepts. Let those who fear You turn to me, those who know Your testimonies. Let my heart be blameless regarding Your statutes, that I may not be ashamed" (Psalm 119:78-80).

It is blatant hypocrisy to preach from a Book that has not been read. As a writer, I get very distressed with persons who write reviews without actually reading my book. If they've read it, they have a right to their opinion, but if they haven't read it, they should keep silent. Merely lifting segments from a book is not grasping the content. Isolated quotes can distort an author's message and unfortunately this is sometimes a deliberate action. Tragically, this is done in the pulpit far more frequently than we would care to admit. If we merely select a quote from one part of the Bible and couple it with a quote from another book in the Bible, we can cause it to say almost anything we want it to say. Simon the sorcerer offered money to Peter and Phillip as payment for his request: "Give me this power also, that anyone on whom I lay hands may receive the Holy Spirit" (Acts 8:18), and Paul wrote, "Now I plead with you, brethren, by the name of our Lord Jesus Christ ... that you be perfectly joined together in the same mind and in the same judgment" (1 Corinthians 1:10). These are accurate quotes from the Bible, but when we place them side by side, we end up teaching the desirability of purchasing Divine power. Many verses cannot be put in juxtaposition without teaching error.

The Premise Stated

Those who would minister the Word of God must fill themselves with that Word, not merely search for proof texts. I am horrified at the great numbers of ministers who have affirmed to me, privately, that they have never read the Bible through once in their entire ministry. They hastily add that they read in the Word, but they have never read it as a book is supposed to be read — from beginning to end. The Bible is not an almanac from which we extract pertinent facts, it is a Book written to reveal God to mankind, and "all Scripture is given by inspiration of God, and is profitable for doctrine, for reproof, for correction, for instruction in righteousness, that the man of God may be complete, thoroughly equipped for every good work" (2 Timothy 3:16, 17). Selected reading will give us limited doctrine and instruction and may well insulate us from reproof and correction. Furthermore, partial reading can only provide partial equipping for ministry.

When speaking to the Lord, Jeremiah could affirm, "Your words were found, and I ate them" (Jeremiah 15:16). He did not say that he preached the words that he found, or quoted them, or wrote them; he declared that he ate them! He became a partaker of the revelation God had allowed him to discover. First, he made it part of his life; then it became a living part of his ministry.

God has not only commanded that His leaders read the Word for themselves; He further has insisted that they read the Word to their followers. He said, "'When all Israel comes to appear before the LORD your God in the place which He chooses, you shall read this law before all Israel in their hearing. Gather the people together, men and women and little ones, and the stranger who is within your gates, that they may hear and that they may learn to fear the LORD your God

and carefully observe all the words of this law' "
(Deuteronomy 31:11, 12). Fearing God is not automatic;
it is acquired. It is not until people know God that they
will have a reverential awe for Him, and the Bible is
God's self-revelation.

Reading the Word aloud to congregations is not
merely an Old Testament principle; it is as New
Testament as the Apostles, for Paul charged the Christians in Colossae, "Now when this epistle is read among
you, see that it is read also in the church of the
Laodiceans, and that you likewise read the espistle
from Laodicea" (Colossians 4:16), and he told the
Thessalonian Christians, "I charge you by the Lord
that this epistle be read to all the holy brethren" (1
Thessalonians 5:27). God's Word needs to be heard.

Just because all Christians in America have access to
a Bible does not mean that they read the Bible. For
many of them, the book remains a mystery, but public
reading of God's Word can often create a taste for the
Bible. Ministers should practice public reading of the
Bible to make it as interesting and important as
anything else they preach. The Bible is not a legal
transcript; it is a love letter, and it should be read as
such.

Ministers should master God's Book, for this is the
major basis of our message. It is the source of our
inspiration, our instruction book, and the revelation of
the God Who has called us into His service. Any claim
to know God without knowing His Word is deceitful.
The purpose of New Testament prophecy is not to
reveal God but to relate us to God; the Bible is the
revelation of God. The exuberance of song is not a
revelation of God; it is a response to a revelation of God.
Nature may declare God, but it is the Bible that
describes Him. For this to be successful, we need more
than a mental appreciation; we need spiritual absorp-
tion of the Book.

The Performance

Systematic reading of God's Word will fill the lives of ministers with the message they are commissioned to share. All too frequently, sermons are mental concepts that have not yet become life principles. Listening to a tape and preaching that concept is not the same as feasting on God's Word and sharing that life. Actually, truth ingested Saturday evening is probably not ready for delivery Sunday morning, any more than food eaten today is muscle and bone tomorrow. We should live the Word before seeking to give the Word. As in the natural, if we eat regularly we will have a constant replenishing of strength, sinew, and bones, so spiritually partaking of the food of God in His Word will renew us in our spiritual nature. Until we become our message, people are hesitant to accept that message. If the truth is not good enough for the minister to eat it, why should it be served to the people? It is unfair for the minister to serve boiled potatoes if he is eating prime rib. We should either eat with the people or let them eat with us.

Ministers need to read the Bible daily. Dr. Howard A Kelly, Professor of Gynecology at Johns Hopkins University from 1889 through 1940, once said, "The very best way to study the Bible is simply to read it daily with close attention and with prayer to see the light that shines from its pages, to meditate upon it, and to continue to read it until somehow it works itself, its words, its expressions, its teachings, its habits of thought, and its presentation of God and His Christ into the very warp and woof of one's being." This daily reading should be devotional in nature. It is not the reading of a student so much as it is the eating of a hungry child.

Ministers also need to read the Bible systematically. We should approach it with a telescope to see distant truth, and scrutinize it carefully with a microscope to behold the many hidden truths within truths. We should read the Bible through at least annually to review its overall theme and to rejoice in its unity in spirit of its having over sixty authors. We should also read the Bible by single books to master the theme, and get to know their historical settings. It will help us catch a glimpse of the individual styles of the authors. Then we are ready to read the Bible chapter by chapter. We should read and reread a chapter until we can outline it with ease. While doing so, we should look for the deeper meaning — the hidden truths — the little "asides" that mean so much. Sometimes reading a variety of translations helps to maintain the freshness of the Word, and mixing our reading in the Old Testament with time spent in the New Testament allows the two testaments to explain each other.

Furthermore, ministers need to study what they have read. We should always make notes when reading the Bible, for often an inspiration of the moment seems so powerful that we expect it to last forever, but it can be lost in a moment. Notebooks, or notes in the margin of our Bibles, will be "self-primers" during dry spells. In our study, we should not be afraid of commentaries and books. God has opened these passages to others; let's see what He said to them. None of us will have all the truth, but each of us has a portion of that truth. Sometimes just one additional piece of the puzzle will help us put the entire picture together. Reach for the puzzle piece God delivered to someone else.

As certainly as ministers need to come regularly to Jesus for a fresh endowment of life through the Spirit, we need to come to the Word for an enlarged revelation of God. Our entire ministry is limited to our comprehension of God. Only time spent in the Word can enlarge that understanding. Anything that successfully keeps us from God's Word also keeps us from knowing

God, and if we do not know Him, we can hardly feast on Him or cause others to feast upon Him.

The Provisions Available

The obvious purpose of consistent reading of God's Word is to fill the life of the minister with the message he is commissioned to share, but there are some excellent byproducts that greatly alter the minister's personal life. The first of these is that the minister filled with God's Word will also be filled with joy. As we saw earlier, Jeremiah, in the midst of the Babylonian seige, with famine and distress all around him, "found and ate" God's words, and exclaimed, "Your word was to me the joy and rejoicing of my heart" (Jeremiah 15:16). Like Jeremiah, today's ministers deal with troubled and often rebellious people. They are often garbage cans for people's emotional distresses, and their personal lives are fraught with stress and heavy responsibilities. Few ministers can find joy in the people they serve, but they can find joy in the Word they eat. Time spent feasting on the Word gives a whole new perspective to life. It affords the Divine overview. God's Word is not a restricter of joy; it is a producer of joy. The psalmist could declare, "Your law is my delight" (Psalm 119:77).

Another by-product of spending time in God's Book is that the minister filled with God's Word will know a life full of Divine peace. The prophet confidently stated, " 'You will keep him in perfect peace, whose mind is stayed on You, because he trusts in You' " (Isaiah 26:3), while the poet said, "Great peace have those who love Your law, and nothing causes them to stumble" (Psalm 119:165). The newspaper may keep us in turmoil, but the Word will keep us in peace. We who minister to others need a stable point of reference in order to relate to this world, and God's Word is the point of reference. When we read it we know Who is in control — we know how it all ends! The Bible is often tomorrow's headlines, for God sees the end from the beginning.

The minister filled with God's Word will experience Divine revelation. It is not the casual reader who discovers deep truths in the Word; it is the consistent student of the Word who uncovers them. Jesus told the disciples, " 'Blessed are your eyes for they see, and your ears for they hear; for assuredly, I say to you that many prophets and righteous men desired to see what you see, and did not see it, and to hear what you hear, and did not hear it' " (Matthew 13:16, 17). God loves to speak to us through His Word, but unless that Word is familiar to us, He is limited in what He can say. It is interesting to see that "new" truth seems to come mostly to those who have a good grasp of "old" truth.

Still another benefit that accrues for faithful readers of the Sacred Page is that the Word-filled minister has a built-in warning against error. David said, "The judgments of the LORD are true and righteous altogether. More to be desired are they than gold, yea, than much fine gold; sweeter also than honey and the honeycomb. Moreover by them Your servant is warned, and in keeping them there is great reward" (Psalm 19:9-11). Doctrinal error comes from not correctly comparing Scripture with Scripture. Knowing the basic theme of the entire Bible keeps us from majoring in minors, which often direct us into error. If we have a clear map of God's pathway, we're not as likely to run down rabbit trails. The more of God's Word we have hidden in our hearts, the less likely we are to get into error. Even improper behavior will trigger an inner warning siren from the Word. Some ministers pride themselves in their extemporaneous speaking, but this demands a thorough knowledge of the Bible lest the speaker wander into false teaching under the guise of "inspiration." Our greatest safety remains in "be[ing] diligent to present [ourselves] approved to God, a worker who does not need to be ashamed, rightly dividing the word of truth" (2 Timothy 2:15).

The psalmist wisely cried out to God, "Your word I have hidden in my heart, that I might not sin against You" (Psalm 119:11). Perhaps if we who minister meditated more in God's Word and less in life's woes we would live more righteously, face less ridicule and be spared much discipline. Inasmuch as we are teaching the Word, we would do well to trust that Word. We need to eat what we serve!

Prayer:

Dear Jesus, Your callings are, indeed, Your enablings, but far too often I have substituted the anointing for preparation of both my heart and my message. Help me to realize that Your anointing is but an energizing of my own self, and it does not give me anything that is not within me. You said that the Spirit would bring all things to my remembrance, but You did not seem to commission Him to put those things in my memory circuits. Lord, forgive my laziness and my preoccupation with things other than Your precious Word, and help me to embrace Your Book as my greatest treasure. Teach me how to feast on it, meditate in it, live with it and in it, and faithfully declare it everywhere I go. I covenant with You, dear Lord, to be a daily partaker of the very food I plan to serve to those whose hearts You have prepared to listen to me minister. Amen.

Chapter 13

Leaders as Producers

"The hard-working farmer must be first to partake of the crops." (2 Timothy 2:6)

When I was a boy in my father's church, I used to enjoy joining the congregation in singing "Hold the Fort." The song pictures the Church desperately holding off an enemy attack awaiting the return of Christ to deliver us from our enemies. It seemed very meaningful at the time, and I suppose that it reminded me of the Indian-pioneer conflicts that pinned the settlers in the fort until the U.S. Cavalry arrived to save them. This siege mentality was popular then, and I fear that it has not entirely gone out of style today. Far too many Christians are just holding on, awaiting Christ's return, but God has not redeemed us to merely maintain the status quo; He has returned authority to the Church so that we can be fruitful producers.

To the standard question "How's it going?" far too many ministers respond with, "Well, we're holding our own." Imagine a business man boasting that he was "breaking even"! Holding our own? Indeed! We should be gaining territory that satan has taken from the Church. We should be increasing in every area of personal living and ministry. Boasting that this year's average attendance equals last year's is to admit that we are losing, not gaining, for the annual population increase in most communities demands growth to even remain constant.

It is great to protect what we have, but God has called us ministers to be far more than mere protectors; we are commissioned to be *producers*. God's kingdom is based on a growth principle. Jesus stated that the work of the kingdom was first the seed, next the sprout, then the head, and finally the ripened grain (*see* Mark 4:28). This speaks of increase based upon life and labor.

The Principle Stated

In his second letter to Timothy, Paul came to grips with this need for ministers to be producers. The theme of chapter two is the rewards of labor, and, having challenged Timothy to be strong, he reminded him, "You therefore must endure hardship" (2 Timothy 2:3). Ministry is difficult, continuous work that has its share of hardship in it. Ministry is not a game or even a profession — it is a Divine calling that the Bible declares involves hard work that demands great discipline and offers great rewards. But rewards in the ministry depend on performance, not on position. It is sad that more graduates from our theological schools seek positions than look for ministerial opportunities. They want title far more than they want toil and they seem unwilling to work to earn a title. A call to the ministry is less a call to position and more a call to work, and work well done affords both rewards and position.

In illustrating this principle of rewards being commensurate with function, Paul used three common illustrations. He spoke first of a soldier in saying,

"You therefore must endure hardship as a good soldier of Jesus Christ" (2 Timothy 2:3), and he then reminded us that complete dedication to the army is mandated when a recruit enlists. All other affairs of life must become subordinate to his soldiering. The army tells him where he will live and what position he will have, and neither he nor his wife can say no! It involves separation, training, danger, and fear, but the soldier is sustained by the thought of final victory.

The second of Paul's illustrations is an athlete. He said, "If anyone competes in athletics, he is not crowned unless he competes according to the rules" (2 Timothy 2:5). Diligent training and self-denial are the lot of the athlete. Everything else in life has to be subordinated to the goal. They deny themselves of many of life's legitimate pleasures and activities in order to better train themselves for the contest. How we need more persons in the ministry whose attitude is "No matter what it costs me, I'll make it!" We must take our share of the hardship if we expect to win the gold medal. The athlete is motivated by the vision of the winner's cup. He dares not entertain the thought of losing, and neither can a minister. We train to win, not to lose!

Finally, Paul spoke of the "hard-working farmer" (2 Timothy 2:6). There is no such thing as a "gentleman-farmer" in the Kingdom of God; we are all hard-working dirt farmers. We do not own a farm that is worked by others; we work a farm that is owned by God. The force that sustains the farmer through months of fruitless toil and constant gamble with the weather is the hope of a harvest, and that same hope should sustain all ministers.

The law of sowing and reaping requires labor first and reaping last. Clearing and plowing precede planting and watering, for all virgin soil is already growing something that must be removed before we plant our crops. Weeding and fertilizing and protecting against predators follow the planting. Anxiety over the weather continues until the crop is actually harvested. Where did we get the idea that we could preach a sermon and have an instant increase? Unless we have entered into the labor of someone else, it is impossible to plow and plant seed in a service and reap a crop with an altar call. James reminded us, "See how the farmer waits for the precious fruit of the earth, waiting patiently for it until it receives the early and latter rain. You also be patient" (James 5:7, 8). Like the child who harvests bean sprouts because the original bean has risen out of the soil instead of allowing the plant to mature and produce a full crop of beans, we often harvest the very seed we planted rather than let it grow, mature, and multiply — which takes more time and labor.

Timothy, and through him the elders in his region, were warned against shirking labor and then expecting to enjoy its fruits. Just as the hard-working person has rights the indolent person has forfeited, so the hard-working minister has rights the slothful minister has forfeited. Ministers are not aristocrats who live off their titles; they are farmers who live off the crops, or shepherds who are dependent upon the increase in the flock, and if there is to be increase, there must be personal investment in labor. Our task is not to preserve our job but to increase the Kingdom.

Since a pastor has full control over his schedule, he can be the laziest man in the community or the busiest. If our concept of the ministry is merely to preach on Sunday, then we can play all week long, but if we see ourselves as farmers or herdsmen fully responsible for the increase in the local congregation, we will put in long, hard hours at our chores.

The Principle Expanded

In saying that "the hard-working farmer must be first to partake of the crops" (2 Timothy 2:6), was Paul saying merely that the farmer should be allowed to eat the firstfruits of the harvest, or was he suggesting that the farmer should be very familiar with and an actual partaker of the very thing that he was planting? *Rotherham's Emphasized New Testament* translates this final phrase, "Ought first of the fruits to partake," which is but a slight difference, yet it implies that before planting the crop in the field, the farmer should have experiential knowledge about that crop. *Gills Commentary* reflects that "the design may be to observe that the ministers of the Word ought first to be partakers of the grace of God, the fruits of the Spirit, and of the gospel, and rightly and spiritually understand it, before they preach it to others." First, we produce it; then we plant it.

The minister cultivates the people, but he plants himself in them. There is a sense, of course, where the Word is the seed, but few hearts have soil that is sufficiently rich or adequately cultivated to cause that seed to sprout. Here in America, we have been scattering seed by radio, television, and preaching for a lengthy season, but the size of the crop is disappointing. It is not the fault of the seed, for God's Word never returns to Him void. Nor should we fault the sower, since many have painstakingly sown the Gospel in diverse fields. Is it possible that we are locked into a system that is almost destined to failure before we begin?

Christ's parable about the sower told of four separate types of ground upon which the seed was scattered. Only one-fourth of the soil brought forth a harvest, and only one-third of that field returned a hundredfold. This means that only one-twelfth of the field gave a bumper crop. If the thirty-fold refers to thirty per cent, then this too would be crop failure. Even sixty per cent return on the seed would not be a very profitable crop for a farmer. In another parable, Jesus spoke of a farmer sowing seed, only to have an enemy come in and plant tares alongside the good seed, creating severe pollution in the crop. Was Jesus trying to discourage us from preaching the Word? Or was He suggesting that there is, perhaps, a more profitable way to produce a healthy crop?

Possibly, this concept (that the farmer should be an initial partaker of the crop he hopes to harvest) might suggest that ministers should sow the Word of God in their own cultivated hearts to produce seedlings that can later be transplanted into the lives of others. Partake first; plant second. There are several advantages of transplanting healthy plants rather than planting seed. The first is that the farmer does not need to be as dependent upon the weather. The seedling can be started in a hothouse long before the fields are ready to be worked. While there are definite seasons in the congregations we pastor, there should never be seasons in the lives of the pastors; we should be prepared to receive the Word at any time, "ready in season and out of season" (2 Timothy 4:2). A second advantage is that the farmer does not need to cultivate an entire field. Landscapers only dig a hole twice the size of the root ball and cultivate and fertilize this small area before transplanting the shrub. It is more realistic financially to completely change the soil for that small section rather than to rework the entire area.

Perhaps we ministers are spending too much time and energy trying to change the soil condition of an entire field when we should be spending more quality time preparing small holes in that field. The seedling already has roots, stalk, and leaves. Once it is planted in proper soil and watered, it will grow. Although seed catalogues still fill our mailboxes each spring, most of us have learned that it is cheaper to purchase bedding plants at the nursery, for our chances of obtaining optimum conditions to germinate that seed into a healthy plant have proved to be very small.

When we allow the Word to produce a crop in our own lives and then watch for opportunities to place one of those seedlings in the life of another, it will not be long before the Church is headed for a harvest, for in taking what has become life in our hearts and imparting it to the heart of another we have imputed that life by transplantation.

The Principle Illustrated

A minister whose heart is filled with missions will develop a church that gets deeply involved in missionary activity. The minister who inwardly grows the crop of faith will impart seedlings from that crop to bring forth a harvest of faith to be planted again and again. Similarly, the person who cultivates worship in his or her life will plant a crop of worship everywhere he or she goes, leaving worshippers in their wake. It is an irrevocable law that what we are growing is what we will reap, and we cannot plant what we do not have. Our congregations become what we are because they will not likely grow what we broadcast in our sermons — they grow what we transplant in them. It is not what we preach, but what we plant, that produces fruit in the lives of others. Therefore, there is little value in preaching grace unless the minister lives it, nor will sermons on love counterbalance a lack of love in the speaker.

The seedlings we ministers transplant are grown in the hothouses of our own lives. The fruit of obedience can be grown in a congregation only if we ministers have the fruit of obedience growing in our own lives. The fruit of the Spirit can be transplanted in another only by a workman who has successfully developed that plant in his own life. Similarly, the gifts of the

Spirit can be transplanted in others only by one who has those gifts sufficiently matured to produce seedlings.

Jesus told His disciples, " 'You did not choose Me, but I chose you and appointed you that you should go and bear fruit, and that your fruit should remain' " (John 15:16).

We are called to bear fruit and then share it. We are ordained not to scatter seed, but to produce fruit and to perpetuate that fruit by transplanting some of the seedlings of truth in the lives of others. Unless we are content with raising annuals, we will have to learn to transplant, for neither orchards nor vineyards are raised from seeds; seasoned stock two or more years old is used in transplanting fruit trees. If we plant the correct root stock, we can have production and harvest year after year without having to replant.

This principle of first raising the stock in our own lives before planting it in others is illustrated in the life of Jesus. As a statement of historic fact, Paul told Timothy, "Remember that Jesus Christ, of the seed of David, was raised from the dead" (2 Timothy 2:8). Christ actually partook of resurrection. To the church at Corinth, Paul gave the doctrinal reason for Christ's resurrection, saying, "But now Christ is risen from the dead, and has become the firstfruits of those who have fallen asleep. For since by man came death, by Man also came the resurrection of the dead. For as in Adam all die, even so in Christ all shall be made alive" (1 Corinthians 15:20-22). First, Christ brought forth the fruit of resurrection; then He raised seedlings so that all believers might have resurrection life living within themselves. The Bible does not teach that we must believe in resurrection life to be raised from the dead; we are taught to believe in the Lord Jesus Christ. The resurrection life is in Him, and He transplants that life into us. We shall be raised from the dead by His action, not by our belief.

The Principle Applied

The order is personal fruit first, then public fruit. It is but another form of the parable of the talents and the pounds, which teaches that God's impartations are given to be multiplied and returned.

The chores of the hardworking farmer are never ended. They are repeated day by day. He is investing himself in his land and his herds and in turn he is rewarded by the increase of his planting. Investment, involvement, toil, patience, and some failure are his lot, but increase is his reward.

Paul added one further admonition to ministers: "Be diligent to present yourself approved to God, a worker who does not need to be ashamed, rightly dividing the word of truth" (2 Timothy 6:15). We receive that Word of truth. We mature that truth within us. We divide that truth into seedlings, and transplant it into prepared hearts. Then in the day of harvest, we need not be ashamed for having been partakers, we will also be producers. Once again the principle is: Ministers, eat what you serve!

Prayer:

Dear Jesus, how many tons of the seed of Your Word I have scattered across the land, with minimal success! Birds, rocks, thorns, and the pressures of life seem to devastate that Word before it can mature in the lives of the hearers. Please help me to grasp the principle of transplanting truth from my experience in God directly into the hearts and lives of persons who will allow their hearts to be spaded and prepared by Your Spirit. May I never forget that Your tree of righteousness in me will never be removed. Only the seedlings that have been produced by this tree can be transplanted, so actually I never lose anything in giving to others. Please grant me the grace of giving so that others may bring forth fruit unto eternal life. Amen!

Chapter 14

Leaders as Praisers

"Praise Him, O you servants of the LORD!"
(Psalm 135:1)

Like the husband working two jobs in order to adequately support his wife and children, many ministers are so busy working for God that they do not have time to enjoy God. Life for them is a ceaseless round of activities and responsibilities that so consume them that they don't know how to simply relax and enjoy the God they serve. Some of this may be rooted in their concepts of God, and much of it is an outgrowth of their own insecurities, but whatever the cause, both God and the minister are being cheated.

David was a great worker for God, but he never let this interfere with his being a worshipper of God as well. His labor was an expression of his love, not a substitute for it. He had all the responsibilities of the kingdom, but he still took time to enjoy the King of kings and the Lord of lords! He never saw himself as a competitor of God; he was always a companion of God.

He preferred to call attention to the Lord rather than to himself. Although totally capable of receiving high honor, David always seemed to prefer to give honor to Jehovah. He was a praiser by nature. He both admired God and enjoyed telling Him so in song, spoken word, and action. He testified, "I will bless the LORD at all times; His praise shall continually be in my mouth" (Psalm 34:1), and this was written at one of the lowest points of his life, as he was hiding in the cave of Adullam while king Saul was seeking to kill him.

Perceiving Praise

Although praise has become quite popular in the past fifteen or so years, many ministers have not yet perceived praise and worship for themselves. They watch members of their congregations or fellowship groups enjoying vocal praise, and they tolerate it, but they do not experience praise welling up in their own spirits. To them, praise is optional, and they often view it as an expression of immaturity. They see praise with their eyes, but they have never grasped it with the senses of their souls and spirits.

Ministers of all categories need to have a firm Bible basis for everything they teach and practice, so seeing praise in the lives of some of the persons for whom they have spiritual responsibility should send them to God's Word, since praise is both an expression of our emotional natures as well as an act of obedience to the clear commands of the Bible. Many hundreds of times we are told to "praise the Lord." Every means of expression that God has built into human nature is to be employed in expressing our love, devotion, and adoration to God. We are instructed to praise God vocally, melodically, physically and continually.

Nevertheless, praise should never be rooted totally in our emotions, for praise is a response to God based upon Who He is, not merely how we feel about Him.

God has commanded us to praise Him, and obedience to that command may or may not be based on erupting feelings at that moment. We must develop the discipline to obey God in spite of our feelings rather than because of them, for if we allow our feelings to control us, we will be at the mercy of our soul rather than under the control of our redeemed spirit.

Seeing praise in the life of another can be very motivational. I'll not forget the deep impression made upon me when, many years ago, I found myself in the presence of a true worshipper of God. It stimulated me to become a praiser and a worshipper, but I soon learned that stimulation was not sufficient motive to make a praiser out of me. I had to search and re-search the Word both for commands to praise and for methods of releasing praise, and I was overwhelmed with the abundance of teaching on praise to be found in virtually every book of the Bible. Praise is expressed in the Psalter, but it is taught and practiced in every division of God's Word.

After seeing praise so indelibly stamped upon the passport into God's presence, I began to try to praise God as I saw others praise Him. I must confess that it was not out of a deep emotional joy, but out of a commitment based upon the clear commands of God. I had seen for myself that praise was the normal expression for a Christian and that it was a commanded expression for God's leader, but that knowledge didn't make obedience any easier. I sometimes praised through gritted teeth. I praised when I felt that everyone was looking at me. I praised in my pulpit even though I felt as conspicuous as though I had arrived without my shirt on. Often my praise was little more than an expression of my desperation, but I had seen praise in the Word, and I was committed to obey that Word.

It was many months before I was genuinely comfortable praising God in front of a congregation, but I continued praising out of disciplined obedience. Eventually, what seemed abnormal became the normal expression of my love for Jesus. I had retrained both my emotions and my will to respond to God the way He has asked us to respond to Him.

God's Word makes no exceptions to the command to praise. No one will ever have an office high enough to exempt him from praise, for the Living Creatures of heaven, likely the highest of God's creation, praise God day and night (*see* Revelation 4:8). Not one of us will ever mature in our relationship with God to a point at which praise is unnecessary, for the Psalmist wrote, and the book of Hebrews quotes Jesus as saying these words: "I will declare Your name to My brethren; in the midst of the congregation I will [sing] praise [to] You" (Psalm 22:22; Hebrews 2:12). If Jesus praised the Father, it must be totally impossible for any of us mortals to mature beyond the need to praise God.

While no minister is exempted from praise, many have not sufficiently perceived praise to bring them out of their resistance to it. Our religious heritages often blind our eyes to clear scriptural truths. We approach God's Word while wearing our doctrinal glasses, which tend to blur our vision to anything that has not been seen clearly by the one who ground our glasses. Praising God is a case in point. One of the first excuses given for nonparticipation in a praise service is, "Our church doesn't do things that way." If that is true, it is sad; but the greatest sorrow is that today's leaders will limit themselves to what yesterday's leaders could see. We need to have our spiritual eyes opened to see what God is showing to the Church in our generation. We need perception that is caused by the teaching of the Word, not blindness that is often produced by dead dogma. When our eyes are opened, our spirits will open to respond, and our souls will open to express the deep praise and worship that has been lying dormant within us for many years.

Preaching Praise

John began his epistle saying, "That which we have seen and heard we declare to you" (1 John 1:3), and Jesus stated, " 'Out of the abundance of the heart the mouth speaks' " (Matthew 12:34). The minister who has finally seen and experienced praise will, of necessity, preach it, teach it, declare it, and share it. What has become life and breath to him will now, through him, become life to others.

Sometimes, however, the minister makes one formal presentation of the need for praise and feels that his or her task has been completed. How quickly we forget how many hours we searched, read, prepared, and studied praise before it was sufficiently embedded in our hearts to actuate praise through us. Most of the people that ministers serve are not keen students of the Word. They are content to let others tell them what the Bible teaches, and they take a little of this and a little of that and form their own life patterns. It takes a lot of telling to effect a change in such people. They need to be told what is going to be told them, then told, and finally be told what they were told. They need a preview, an overview, and a review if any change is to be produced in them.

When I came into praise, I desperately wanted the congregation I was then serving to come into praise with me. I preached praise in nearly every service for over a year. Persons would approach my sister, Iverna Tompkins, who was then serving as my associate, to ask, "Doesn't your brother know anything other than praise?" Her answer was, "Of course he does, but quite obviously he is going to keep on this subject until we do it!"

It is never sufficient for people to merely be exposed to praise; they must be initiated into it. We must tell it, teach it, and then urge them to try it, for praise requires more than intellectual consent — it demands action! After preaching on praise, I used to gather the congregation at the front of the auditorium and lead them in a practice session. Initially, they were as self-conscious as I had been in my beginning praise, but practice not only makes perfect — it builds confidence.

Obviously, ministers must become praisers before we can lead others into praise, but once we have sufficiently renounced our pride to be able to publicly praise the Lord, we should begin to gently but consistently lead our followers into praise.

Besides bringing people into a joyful release of their emotions to God, preaching praise has other benefits. Foremost among them may well be that praising forces a congregation into positive attitudes. So many of our people live in a negative world. They are constantly aware of the stress of life, the loneliness of life's relationships, and the pain of their physical bodies. When we get them to take their gaze off themselves to fix their sight upon the Lord, we lead them into a release that brings healing to the entire being. Praise is positive prayer that causes us to deal with God instead of with the problem, the devil, or even ourselves. Rather than lead a congregation in rebuking satan, it is far more valuable to lead them into rejoicing in God. God can deal with the devil far more effectively than we can, and He will if we consistently give Him the glory and honor that is due His name.

Still another good byproduct of bringing others into praise is the release through them of a flow that will begin as a vertical response, but will soon become a horizontal expression as well. People that praise together soon find themselves loving one another. Many of the emotional wounds and hurts that were produced by the week's activities will be healed by the flow of love that overwhelms a praising congregation. This will not be the artificial handshake that has become the hallmark of religion — it will be the filial love brothers and sisters have one for another because of their common parentage. As a pastor I saw more persons healed emotionally during united praise than in the counselling chambers, for praise deals with God, brings us into positive emotional responses, and it introduces us into the flow of God's love. That is the basis of emotional health.

Praise cannot become the only thing that is proclaimed, for all congregations need a balanced diet, but praise is so important that it should be worked into nearly every message some way. If praise is systematically proclaimed and regularly demonstrated in every service, it will become the accepted norm, not the random response of emotional stimuli. Praising God is the main purpose of public assembly of Christians, but it must be taught by a minister who has caught it.

Practicing Praise

It is, of course, one thing to see and preach praise, and quite another thing to practice praise in daily behavior. By virtue of our calling as ministers of the Gospel, we are far more apt to hear negatives and be involved with problems than to hear positive reports and be given praise. Humans that we are, we find ourselves in a negative state of mind more often than we desire. It is difficult to preach a positive Gospel from a negative spirit, but many of us have desperately tried. It is true that we have been charged to "weep with those who weep," but we have also been commanded to "rejoice with those who rejoice" (*see* Romans 12:15). The discipline that was necessary to bring us into praise responses must be exercised to keep us living a life of praise.

About two years after my first book, *Let Us Praise*, had been released, I came into a set of circumstances that seriously depressed me. Hoping to find consolation, I attended a morning prayer meeting in a local congregation that really knew how to pray. I had purposed to tell all of my feelings to them and to explain the reasons for those feelings, but at the very beginning of the service, I was introduced to a guest minister to whom I was a stranger. I didn't want to bare my soul in front of him, so I purposed to outpray him. But even when he finished praying, he stayed in the prayer room, so in desperation, I repressed my pride and exposed myself to these saints. Before the pastor could respond in any way, the guest spoke up asking, "Didn't you say your name was Cornwall?"

"Yes," I replied.

"Are you the Judson Cornwall who wrote the book on praise?"

"That's me," I admitted.

"You don't need prayer," he said. "You just need to practice what you wrote."

The pastor began to rebuke the minister, but I intervened by saying, "I believe that the Lord spoke to me through this brother." How easy it is to forget the things we have written, preached, and counselled others to do. But it is not what we know or can communicate, but what we can put into operation in our own lives that transforms us into the image of God.

It is highly improbable that the victory in our lives will be able to rise any higher than our consistent praising. Things may go wrong, but God is changeless. Praise the Lord! People can be cruel and thankless, but God is consistently loving and kind. Praise the Lord! The problems we face are far beyond our abilities, but nothing is greater than God's omnipotence, so praise the Lord! We need to get a permanent hold on the upward look, for it is the only sensible direction to look in the midst of a storm. If you doubt that, ask Noah!

Of the Pharisees — the most fundamental religious group in the days of Jesus — John wrote, "They loved the praise of men more than the praise of God" (John 12:43). Each of us who has accepted the responsibility of ministry must guard our spirits constantly lest our desire to be praised overrides our desire to praise God and to lead others into praise. A little praise is heady wine, and a flattering praise can totally scramble our brains. We must learn to direct all praise back to the Lord without tasting it, lest we develop an appetite for it and direct people's attention to ourselves rather than to the Person of God.

Ministers are due honor and respect, but all glory and praise must go to God, Who has called us into His glorious ministry.

David cried, "You who fear the LORD, praise Him!" (Psalm 22:22). The Hebrew word we have translated for "fear" is *yaw-ray*, which forms the root of our word *revere*. Not only do we reverence the Lord, we allow ourselves to be called "reverend." Certainly we should be the first to praise the Lord. We absolutely must eat what we serve!

Prayer:

Dear Lord Jesus, You have opened my eyes to see the place, power and performance of praise both in my individual life and in the lives of the people to whom I minister. Please prevent me from doing anything that would draw this praise to myself, and teach me to live the life of a worshipper of God so that Your praises will always fill my heart and flow out of my mouth. Thank You for this. Amen!

Chapter 15

Leaders as Physicians

"Is there no physician there?" (Jeremiah 8:22)

We live in a sick world! The disease of sin is far more than miserable; it is fatal. Nationally, internationally and individually, this infirmity has passed epidemic stages. One does not need to be exposed to this sickness to catch the affliction, for it seems to be inherited at birth. Its symptoms are diverse, and its debilitating effects work at different paces in separate individuals, but the results are both catastrophic.

Generations of people have sought a cure for it. Medical doctors spend their lives treating the symptoms and seeking cures, but as soon as an antidote for one manifestation of the sickness is found, this pestilence merely creates a whole new set of symptoms. It is baffling to medical science.

Those who deal with the science of the mind have tried for many years to convince people that this malady does not actually exist. They blame it upon outdated Victorian values, projected religious guilt, and lack of full acquaintance with one's inner self. They are frequently successful in convincing people that they are not ill, but the morticians bury their bodies just the same.

The great tragedy in our enlightened society is that this malady is curable. The failure of medicinal and psychological science to find this cure is rooted in the fact that they think the sickness is in the body or the soul of people, when it actually is deep within man's spirit. Spiritual sickness warps the soul and wounds the body, but merely treating the twisted soul or the deformed body does not confront the disease hidden deep in the spirit.

Spiritual disease can only be treated in the spirit, by spiritual means. Christ Jesus is the only answer to the problem of sin and its incumbent sickness. Where He and His cross are applied, the disease of sin is destroyed. This is the only known cure for sin, and the only cure that mankind will ever require. The greatest need in the world today is not for surgeons, physicians, pharmacists, or disease-control specialists. The world desperately needs ministers who know how to apply God's remedy to the problem of sin — those who can apply the healing balm of Gilead (*see* Jeremiah 8:22). If we do not effectively come to grips with this sickness, men and women will die in their sin.

Physicians of the Spirit

God made us for communion and fellowship with Himself. Since " 'God is Spirit' " (John 4:23), He, naturally enough, communes and fellowships with us in our spirits. When our spirits are in right relationship with the Father, His very life flows in and through us, but if something severs that flow, our spirits begin to sicken, weaken, and die. God alone is the Source of life for our spirits. To the religious leaders of His day, Jesus said, "You search the Scriptures, for in them you think you have eternal life; and these are they which testify of Me. But you are not willing to come to Me that you may have life" (John 5:39, 40). Spiritual life is neither in doctrine nor in dogma. It is in God Himself, and it can be received only directly from Him.

Sin severs the relationship between our spirits and God's Spirit. The prophet stated, "Your iniquities have separated you from your God; and your sins have hidden His face from you, so that He will not hear" (Isaiah 59:2). Just as Adam's sin surrendered his right to the Tree of Life and induced his expulsion from the Garden and from God's presence, so our sin produces a death-dealing separation from God, our Tree of Life.

No amount of religious exercise will restore life to the spirit that has been separated from God. Healing can come only if there can be restoration with God. Since we were unable to initiate this renewed relationship, God Himself inaugurated it through the death of Christ at Calvary. Paul explained it by saying, "That God was in Christ reconciling the world to Himself, not imputing their trespasses to them, and has committed to us the word of reconciliation" (2 Corinthians 5:19). God handled sin through the substitutionary, vicarious sacrifice of Jesus, and He has commissioned His ministers to tell the world that mankind may once again plug their spirits into God and draw everlasting life from Him.

It is in this sense that ministers are physicians of the spirit. We not only understand the nature and cause of the disease, but we know the cure. Once sin is handled, fellowship is restored, and the life that flows from God restores the sickened spirit to fullness and health. Ours is the good news. We are heralds of life, for we are proclaimers of the Gospel of reconciliation and restoration.

God has not called us to accommodate people in their sin, but to call men and women to repentance so that there can be a remission of sin unto salvation of their dying spirits. This demands a crisis confrontation with self and with God, but, painful as this may be, nothing short of this will ever bring healing to the spirits of dying people.

Teaching people to accept themselves as they are is a death-dealing substitute for teaching them to accept the finished work of Christ on their behalf. Enduring sin is a suicide mission. Sin must be removed from the human spirit or death will reign over every area of a person's life. Ask any drug addict! God give us more ministers who will say with Paul, "I am not ashamed of the gospel of Christ, for it is the power of God to salvation for everyone who believes" (Romans 1:16).

Physicians of the Soul

In man's spirit, he has God-consciousness, but in his soul he has self-consciousness. It is in his soul that he has intellect and emotions, and it is through his soul that he establishes and fulfills relationship with others. Because the Scriptures often interchange the terms "soul" and "spirit," we ministers often speak of God saving souls, as though the soul were the seat of sin. But sin is an act of the will that separates a person from God, and as such, sin is an act of the spirit that deeply affects the soul. We know, of course, that we can separate the two of these only theologically, for the soul/spirit are so integrated that successful separation of the two is impossible.

Sin, which has cut off our relationship with God, also deeply affects our relationships with others. Our churches are filled with people who are wounded because of bad and broken relationships with other persons. Some have been so violated by others that they cannot trust even God. People live with wounded souls that consistently produce sobs in the night and fears in the daytime. We ministers dare not ignore this.

The world has no healing for these wounds. It offers amusement to take our minds off our hurts, and it offers drugs to anesthetize our senses so we don't feel the pain, but it cannot heal the damage. Only the Gospel can do this. Ministers have the only healing word for today's maimed souls. Where else can an addict find both physical and emotional healing? The confused, unwed, pregnant teenager needs healing for her soul as well as guidance in handling her pregnancy. The Gospel message of love and acceptance is a healing balm for this plus thousands of similar emotional crises.

For many ministers the term "inner-healing" has a negative connotation, but sin has so damaged men and women's inner nature that healing is needed. A wise minister can bring these hurting persons to Christ and stand by while Jesus makes the person whole again. The intervention of a minister can often reestablish relationships that have deteriorated through sin and can also guide persons into healthy relationships to replace broken affiliations.

It has been said that the three most damaging emotions in the human soul are fear, anger, and guilt. We ministers have practical answers to all three of these. David told us how he handled fear: "I will fear no evil; for You are with me; Your rod and Your staff, they comfort me" (Psalm 23:4). David had numerous occasions for fear, and he did not deny the presence of that emotion, but he refused to give in to it because he knew that he was not alone in the circumstance. God was with him! Like the child who trusts the father for security, David trusted God at all times. So can we!

It is Paul who gave us an answer to the powerful emotion of anger. He wrote, "Beloved, do not avenge yourselves, but rather give place to wrath; for it is written, 'Vengeance is Mine, I will repay,' says the Lord. 'Therefore if your enemy hungers, feed him; if he thirsts, give him a drink; for in so doing you will heap coals of fire on his head' " (Romans 12:19, 20). If God is going to repay evildoers, we do not have to find a way to get even with them. We can let the healing emotion of love flow through us, and leave the dangerous emotion of anger to God.

We ministers also have an answer to the destructive emotion of guilt, for we can take the guilt-ridden persons to the Bible and show them that their sins were forgiven in Christ at Calvary and that "there is therefore now no condemnation to those who are in Christ Jesus" (Romans 8:1). The sinner cannot be his own judge. God is the judge of all men, and only the judge can hand down the guilty verdict. If God says, "Forgiven," then there can be no condemnation. We need but forgive ourselves as God, for Christ's sake, has forgiven us.

In speaking of the Good Shepherd, the Psalmist said, "He restores my soul" (Psalm 23:3). Should not we undershepherds do similarly? Emotions need to be healed. Trust must be rebuilt. Fellowship with others must be reactivated, and self-confidence must be restored. The souls of people who have been redeemed need to be revitalized. It is a healing ministry God has entrusted to His chosen servants. We need to accept our appointment as physician of the soul.

Physician of the Body

When the spirit or the soul is ill, the body usually manifests the symptoms, for the body is the channel of expression and the medium of relating to the world for both the soul and the spirit. As such, it is virtually the slave of the higher nature, and it is also subject to the sicknesses of the soul and the spirit. Many doctors recognize that a high percentage of the physical ailments they treat in people are caused by problems in the inner person. My oldest daughter, who is a nurse, once worked for a doctor who would give his patients prescriptions for medicinal drugs, telling them that this would treat their symptoms. Then he would ask them who they hated, or what the basis of their inner resentment was, after which he would give them three Bible verses to be memorized as a treatment for the cause of their illness. His rate of cures was amazingly high, for he refused to treat the body as a separate entity from the soul and spirit.

Immediately after Israel crossed through the Red Sea, God confronted his covenant people and said, "If you diligently heed the voice of the LORD your God and do what is right in His sight, give ear to His commandments and keep all His statutes, I will put none of the diseases on you which I have brought on the Egyptians. For I am the LORD who heals you" (Exodus 15:26). *Jehovah-Rapha* is the compound Hebrew name used here for God. "God — the Physician," or "God — Who heals" would be a literal translation for this name of God. It is the nature of God to heal, not to afflict. Jesus testified, " 'He has sent Me to heal the broken-hearted' " (Luke 4:18), and His ministry was filled with many acts of healing.

Throughout the Bible, healing is viewed as affecting the whole man. Scholars contend that the statement "By His stripes we are healed" (Isaiah 53:5) refers to the healing of the entire person — spirit, soul and body — but most commentators and current preachers seem to leave out any provision for the body. It is popular in many religious circles to denounce "Divine healing," claiming that there is no positive proof of anyone being healed through prayer. They are wrong, of course, for thousands of people can give an honest testimony to God's intervention to arrest physical disease and cure sickness.

In the Old Testament, Moses was instructed to erect a bronze serpent on a pole. Anyone suffering and dying from the bite of the poisonous vipers needed only to look at it — that erected symbol of Christ who would later become our sin and die the death we deserved in order to free us from the venomous bite of sin — to be instantly healed. The prophetic books record instances of people being healed and even raised from the dead, and king Hezekiah was Divinely healed from a fatal malady through the intervention of the prophet Isaiah. *Jehovah-Rapha* was active on behalf of His people in the Old Testament.

The four Gospels and the book of Acts abound with records of healings performed instantly by God in response to the faith of individuals here on earth. Healing is a provision of God for all the effects of sin in a person. What we do not know about Divine healing probably greatly exceeds what we do know, but our ignorance about it does not prevent it from happening. Perhaps our greatest mistake is in trying to reduce Divine healing to a doctrine with laws of application. Divine healing is in a Person. Jesus Christ is God's provision for sin-sick mankind. He, and He alone, is the healer of our spirits, souls, and bodies. If we would side-step our doctrinal teaching that tries to put healing in a definable box, and just bring the sick person to Jesus, much as the four friends did when they let the palsied man down through the roof, we would see more people completely healed.

If we allow our lack of understanding of how Divine healing works keep us from praying for the sick, God will find someone who will believe His Word and His Divine provision to make men whole, for He is a compassionate God Who can "sympathize with our weaknesses" (Hebrews 5:15). The fear of failure that keeps many ministers from praying for the sick is usually rooted in a subconscious feeling that the minister is responsible for the requested healing, but this is not so. We are merely responsible to respond to requests for prayer. Christ Jesus is the healer. The options are all His, and He seems to delight in exercising those options in such diverse ways as to keep us from formulating rules by which we expect Him to abide.

Cosmetic Physicians

God has not called ministers to cover the sins of people with verbal cosmetics. Sin is not a simple blemish on the face; it is a disease in the spirit. We may hide the pimple on the surface, but until we eradicate the disease that flows through the individual, there will be more and more eruptions that call for more and more cosmetics. Making people look better is not God's goal. Making people whole is the purpose of the cross.

On one occasion, God cried, " 'From the prophet even to the priest, everyone deals falsely. They have also healed the hurt of My people slightly, saying "Peace, peace!" when there is no peace. Were they ashamed when they had committed abomination? No! They were not at all ashamed; Nor did they know how to blush. Therefore they shall fall among those who fall; at the time I punish them, they shall be cast down,' says the LORD" (Jeremiah 6:13-15). These ministers were telling the people what they wanted to hear even though it was contrary to what God was saying. They were "slightly" healing the wound of the people, but it was little more than a cosmetic application.

Giving people hope is a tremendous healing grace, but giving persons a false hope will increase their hurts rather than heal them. We ministers need to deal honestly with the problem of sin and sickness. There is no room for deceit or hypocrisy in our ministry, nor is there need for it. God is the Great Physician Who can totally heal, but sometimes He functions as the surgeon who, in removing a diseased organ, temporarily makes us sicker in order to make us whole.

We ministers dare not treat sin lightly. Survival in

life and eternal destinies are at stake. Slightly removing a symptom is not healing. We must bring people to genuine confession of sin and acceptance of Christ the Savior. Perhaps a little more time spent in the conversion process would mean much less time in the counseling chambers later. If we get rid of the cause we will not have to treat the symptoms.

Jesus quoted a proverb that was as familiar in His day as it is in ours: "Physician, heal yourself!" (Luke 4:23). How sad it is to see the news magazines and the television talk-shows chronicling the moral illnesses of some of those who have ministered to the multitudes. The projection is valid: "If it won't work for you, why proclaim it to us?" There has never been a time when it was more important for ministers to eat what they serve.

Prayer:

Dear Lord, I am constantly surrounded by sick people, and the compassion of my heart reaches out to them. Please help me to take my position as a minister of God and introduce these people to Jesus the Healer — Jehovah-Rapha. Forgive me for all my attempts at cosmetic surgery, and help me to deal with sin as the root cause of our problems. People don't know You, but I know You, so they look to me as the physician. Help me to keep this in perspective and to bring them with their sicknesses to the foot of the cross so that You can heal them. Amen!

Chapter 16

Leaders as Porters

"The Son of man ... commanded the porter to watch"
(Mark 13:34, KJV)

The term *porter* often brings to mind the image of natives carrying the white hunter's possessions on their heads as they cut their way through the thick African jungle to the sound of chattering monkeys and roaring lions. In a more civilized setting, we visualize the old railroad depot with the coal-burning engine chugging away, belching steam and smoke as it drags a string of Pullman coaches to the loading platform; amid the sound of shrill train whistles comes the repeated cry of "Porter!" as uniformed, red-capped men hurry to carry passengers' luggage to and from the train.

Actually, both of these pictures are applicable to the pastor. He is certainly a burden-bearer; his responsibility includes helping persons on their journey into God, and handling their luggage is part of the job. Marriage counseling, family planning, budget help, and baby dedications may not seem to be very spiritual, but weary travelers must get through to God with all of it, and frequently they need a lot of assistance. The pastor, like the Son of Man, comes not to be served but to serve and to give his life for others (*see* Matthew 20:28).

In reality, however, neither of these pictures of burden-bearers even comes close to depicting what the Bible word *porter* actually means. The Hebrew word we translate as *porter* is *show'er*, meaning "door-keeper," and the Greek word is *thuroros*, which is a combination of *thura*, "a door," and *ourous*, "a guardian." In the Bible, then, a porter is always a doorkeeper or gatekeeper. Even our English word "porter" comes from the Latin word *portarius*, "the man who attended the portal, the gate." Accordingly, the New King James Bible consistently translates this word as "gatekeeper."

The Place of a Porter

Because of the high defensive value of gates, gatekeepers held an honorable and highly respected position in Israel. In the days of King David, the gatekeepers ("porters," KJV) were chosen from the Levite priests, particularly from among the sons of Korah, Asaph, and Obed-Edom (*see* 1 Chronicles 26). These were not ordinary men chosen for guard duty; the Bible record says that they were "men of great ability," "able men with strength for the work," and "among the chief men, having duties just like their brethren, to serve in the house of the LORD" (1 Chronicles 26:6, 8, 12).

These men were chosen because of demonstrated abilities and spiritual stature. They are not spoken of as being tall, or physically muscular, but as being men "with strength for the work." Sometimes the "iron-pumpers" with the showy physiques will not use that strength in common labor. God needs workmen, not showmen. The chosen gatekeepers were men not merely of great ability, but also of great dreams. They more than talked a good defense — they possessed the ability to implement good plans in practical everyday living. May God give us more men like this to keep the gates!

These men who were given gatekeeping responsibilities were men who had already learned to serve God. First, they were chosen from among the Levitical priests, whose main purpose in life was the service of God. Second, these families had already been appointed by David "to minister before the ark of the LORD, to commemorate, to thank, and to praise the LORD God of Israel ..." (1 Chronicles 16:4-6). They were special servants of God, so it was easy for them to serve God's children in a special way. Happy is the congregation whose minister knows how to "minister before the Lord," for worshippers always make the best gatekeepers.

That they enjoyed this service is evident from the psalms of the sons of Asaph and Korah. Asaph himself wrote, "It is good for me to draw near to God; I have put my trust in the Lord God, that I may declare all your works" (Psalm 73:28), but one of the sons of Korah became even more specific when he wrote, "How lovely is Your tabernacle, O LORD of hosts! My soul longs, yes, even faints for the courts of the LORD: my heart and my flesh cry out for the living God. I would rather be a doorkeeper in the house of my God than dwell in the tents of wickedness" (Psalm 84:1, 2, 10).

If the Old Testament porters were men of ability, strength, leadership and spiritual maturity, should not the New Testament gatekeepers be all this and more? Paul's list of qualifications for bishops and deacons (*see* 1 Timothy 3:1-13) would seem to say so! Those who become the guardians of the way into God's city and God's presence must be extraordinary persons with leadership ability and spiritual maturity, or our enemy will capture our gates and have full access to our cities. While it is true that these gatekeepers were servants, both of the Lord and of the people, it is obvious that they were highly qualified servants.

The Purpose of a Porter

The role of the gatekeeper was at least threefold. He was the watchman for the city; he was the city's first line of defense; and he controlled access to the city. Certainly persons in ministry, especially pastors, have these same responsibilities.

The first role of the gatekeeper was the most obvious one. He was the watchman for the city. Frequently, he sat high on the city walls in a small booth over the gate of his charge, which gave him a perspective far greater than any resident in the city could have. Although Jerusalem had twelve gates, David divided the gatekeepers into four groups to man the east, north, south, and west gates (*see* 1 Chronicles 26:13-16). Obviously their first function was to be watchmen.

When God was explaining the role He expected His servant to play, He told Ezekiel, " 'So you, son of man: I have made you a watchman for the house of Israel; therefore you shall hear a word from My mouth and warn them for Me' " (Ezekiel 33:7). Ministers are gatekeeper-watchmen. The enemy of the Church does not always attack in broad daylight with a shouting army; he often creeps up in the night seasons with a camouflaged company of highly trained experts whose goal is to control a gate of entrance to the city for the army that waits to attack. Ministers of the Gospel have an elevated position on the walls that affords them a larger perspective of what is going on, and God holds them responsible to see, rightly interpret what they see, and sound a warning to the sleeping inhabitants in the protected city. The people's safety is in our hands.

If we don't recognize the enemy in the darkness, the city may well be overthrown.

This makes the watchman the city's first line of defense. He not only warns others of impending danger, but at the first sign of enemy action, he uses his position and strength to close and secure the gates against an attack, for the enemy can best be defeated if he is kept outside the walls.

Ministers are responsible before God to keep the enemy outside the city walls, for if he gains access to the city, there will be severe casualties even among the noncombatants. When the gate of sexual purity is left unattended, a church suffers an invasion that devastates the marriages and homes in that congregation. Similarly, when the gate of doctrinal integrity is left open to enemy invasion, the congregation's faith can be diluted, polluted, or even destroyed.

We ministers need to know that as gatekeepers, we are the first line of defense for the people we serve. Jesus spoke of Himself as " 'the door of the sheep' " (John 10:7) and said, " 'The good shepherd gives His life for the sheep' " (John 10:11). The allusion is to the stone enclosures in the pasture into which the sheep were herded at nightfall. The shepherd lay down in the opening to this enclosure, thereby effectively becoming the door, or gate, to the enclosure. No predator could get to the sheep without first getting by the shepherd, nor could a sheep slip out of the enclosure without waking the shepherd. What an example for those of us who are entrusted with the ministry of gatekeeping!

But as vital as the roles of watchman and defender were, the primary duty of a gatekeeper was to control entrance to and exit from the city. He determined who went into and out of the city. When Nehemiah was angry with the men of Tyre for coming to Jerusalem to sell their merchandise on the Sabbath, he commanded that the gates be shut for the entire Sabbath day, and he posted his own servants at the gates to enforce this edict (*see* Nehemiah 13:16-21). He was controlling entrance to the city.

Conversely, when Joshua's two spies were discovered in Jericho, the first thing the elders of the city did was to command that the gates be shut (*see* Joshua 2:5). The same thing happened to Samson in Gaza (*see* Judges 16:2, 3). These elders were controlling all exiting from the city.

God spoke through the prophet Isaiah regarding a future day of restoration when " 'they shall call you the City of the LORD, Zion of the Holy One of Israel ... you shall call your walls Salvation, and your gates Praise' " (Isaiah 60:14, 18). Many scholars see this as a prophetic reference to the New Testament Church. God has assembled His covenant people, the Church, within the protective walls of Divine Salvation, and entrance to and exit from this sanctuary are through the gates of Praise.

Since it is the gatekeeper who controls the gates, it becomes the responsibility of the ministers of the Gospel to open the gates of praise that allow the people to come into the presence of God. David understood this role of the gatekeepers, for he wrote, "Lift up your heads, O you gates! And be lifted up, you everlasting doors! And the King of glory shall come in" (Psalm 24:7). In calling for the opening of the gates, David visualized God Himself coming into the presence of His covenant people.

Whether we think of God coming to us or us coming into God's presence, the gates of praise absolutely must be opened, and the gatekeeper controls the gates. Ministers, especially pastors, must lead their people in praise and worship. While he may not always be the person at the microphone, the pastor, as spiritual leader of his congregation, must be an active participant in the worship service, or his people will not enter in through the praise gate. Some leaders delegate this responsibility to a layman or staff member and then sit back reviewing their sermon notes or talking with an usher on a phone. The people are conscious of the pastor's nonparticipation, and their attitude may very well be "If he isn't going to go through this gate, why should we?"

While it may not be necessary for the gatekeeper to actually pull the ropes that lift the gates, he is the one who gives the order, and he should be vitally concerned with every phase of the operation. If the ministry of a soloist or an ensemble isn't important enough to warrant the pastor's attention, it shouldn't be on the program in the first place, and if praise doesn't merit the participation of the pastor, it shouldn't be a part of the service. Release the worshippers to attend a church where praise and worship are more than a preliminary or a religious game!

The Procrastination of a Porter

As with all other roles, it is possible to get so caught up in the responsibilities of gatekeeping that we fail to properly protect ourselves. Some watchmen faithfully warn others of impending danger without doing anything about it personally. It becomes a case of, "Do what I say, not what I do." They do not make adjustments in their own lives in light of an approaching enemy. They faithfully close defensive gates for others while leaving the same gates open in their own lives. They courageously defend others from a common enemy without actually defending themselves. Perhaps it is through a perverted sense of duty to others, or maybe it is the love of daring, but most likely it is mere procrastination. "Tomorrow" is often one of the enemy's best weapons. Paul reminded us, "Behold, now is the day of salvation" (2 Corinthians 6:2). If a minister is ever going to protect himself from a destructive attack of the enemy, it must be now, not later. Sounding the alarm is good, but heeding that alarm is better. What will the city do if the gatekeeper falls to an enemy?

Some of the harshest words Jesus ever used are recorded in Matthew 23. In His denunciation of the religious leaders of His day, he said, " 'Woe to you, scribes and Pharisees, hypocrites! For you shut up the kingdom of heaven against men; for you neither go in yourselves, nor do you allow those who are entering to go in' " (v. 13). Unfortunately, this is as common today as it was then. From the days of Christ until now, it has been the religious gatekeepers who have hindered people from entering into a personal relationship with God. Like the proverbial dog in a manger, they will not eat, nor will they allow the cattle to partake of the grain. It is bad enough that they have refused to enter into such a life, but their condemnation is all the worse for prohibiting others from coming to God's fullness.

Somehow spiritual gatekeepers seem to feel that they must either protect God from people or protect people from God, for they consistently keep the gates into the Divine presence closed and barred. God does not need to be defended — He is perfectly capable of self-defense and people do not need to be protected from God — they need His presence in their lives. The psalmist says, "This is the gate of the LORD, through which the righteous shall enter" (Psalm 118:20). We are porters for gates of entrance, not keepers for the gates of exclusion. One who hungered after God said, "Open to me the gates of righteousness; I will go through them, and I will praise the LORD" (Psalm 118:19). He had learned what we need to know: Ministers, eat what you serve!

Prayer:

Heavenly Father, You have made me a keeper of the gates. Make me a wise watchman who takes personal precautions while making public proclamations of impending danger. May I not be like Rhoda, the doorkeeper in the book of Acts, who failed to open the gate to let Peter come into the fellowship and protection of the saints. Cause me to faithfully open the gates of praise and lead Your people through that opened portal right into Your glorious presence. If I refuse to enter, or if I try to prevent others from entering, remove me from this office and replace me with a porter who wants Your presence more than he wants life itself. Amen!

Chapter 17

Leaders as Provokers

"Provoke unto love and to good works"
(Hebrews 10:24, KJV)

In some ways, the politician and the pastor are very
much alike. Getting elected (or appointed) requires
shaking hands and kissing babies, but getting the job
done often demands twisting arms and kicking back-
sides. While their job security may rest on pleasing the
people, the very nature of their work often provokes
their constituents.

Today's emphasis upon a happy, magnetic personality for a minister together with a ministry that
pleases and pacifies the people is a far cry from the
Bible examples of the persons God chose to lead His
people. Those men and women were consistent goads
to the conscience, challenges to the status quo, and
provocations to righteousness. You could actually call
them "blessed troublemakers." Moses walked into
Egypt and totally rearranged life for both the Israelites

and the Egyptians. Deborah provoked Israel to a successful battle against the Canaanites; Gideon incited Israel to overthrow the Midianites; and Elijah closed the heavens, producing a three-year drought. Few, if any, of the prophets were popular in their generation, for they proclaimed a word from God that often cut across the grain of the lives of kings and princes. Certainly, Jesus was a thorn to everyone but the common people. His birth caused an uproar in Herod's palace and all Jerusalem. His ministry was a constant threat to the religious leaders, and His crucifixion sounded the death knell for the powers of hell.

None of these servants of God sought to be obnoxious, but each had a message and a ministry that discovered deceit, exposed sin, revealed righteousness, and challenged people to change. For good cause, religion and politics have consistently viewed true men and women of God as troublemakers, for they are heavenly minded, morally motivated, and uncompromisingly true to what they have seen and heard in God. These persons may see themselves as ministers, but the world views them as meddlers.

Rejection by the world is to be expected. As a matter of fact, Jesus warned us, " 'Woe to you when all men speak well of you, for so did their fathers to the false prophets' " (Luke 6:26). Few true ministers need to worry about being fully accepted by those outside the covenant community of believers, but most of us desire to be embraced by this brotherhood. Often our need for acceptance is so great that we compromise our ministry in exchange for popularity. This may fulfill our self-images and satisfy our egos, but the cost to the lives of the people we claim to lead may be more than it is worth. God has called us not as pacifiers but as provokers. We have been called into the ministry, not for our well-being, but for the maturation of the saints.

This demands the use of many skills and tools, among which is provoking.

The Way We Provoke

God's Word challenges us, "Let us consider one another to provoke unto love and to good works" (Hebrews 10:24, KJV). The Greek word chosen by the Holy Spirit and translated "provoke" is *paroxusmos*, which *Young's Concordance* defines as "contention, or incitement to good." To this, W. E. Vine added "stimulation."

God expects His ministers to contend with persons to strive for excellence. He wants us to incite them to good works and to stimulate them to love. We're more than proclaimers of what is right; we are provokers to righteous behavior.

When my daughters lived at home, they would often get upset at my unwillingness to answer a question directly. Usually, I would ask them a series of questions that would help them discover the answer for themselves, or I would direct them to a book in my library that would tell them what they wanted to know. To their resistance I would command, "Think!" It would have been far easier to merely tell them what they wanted to know, but learning to think was far more important than learning facts. I provoked them to thinking, and they have repeatedly thanked me for it in later life.

In our everyday speech, "provoke" usually has a negative connotation. If a person irritated us, we say, "He provoked me." The word is widely used in this sense in the Scriptures, but some passages, such as Hebrews 10:24, use it very positively. To further enhance this distinction, the New King James Bible translates it, "Let us consider one another in order to stir up love and good works." Provoking is "stirring up." What is stirred up determines whether it is positive or negative.

Ministers who are responsible for the spiritual welfare of others should refuse to be satisfied with mediocrity. We dare not allow our people to settle for less than God's best. We must inspire them to greatness and influence them for godliness. If it becomes necessary, we can even irritate them to change and incite them to action. Like the frog who will submit to being boiled alive if you start him in cold water and raise the temperature gradually, people will accommodate their circumstances without even considering a redemptive change. Spiritual leaders need to consistently challenge and even cajole their followers to adjust for the better.

The Greek word *paroxusmos* is the root of our English word paroxysm, which the *Merriam-Webster New Collegiate Dictionary* defines as "a fit, attack, or sharp increase in intensity; any sudden, violent action or emotion; a convulsion or fit." Sometimes, we need to provoke persons almost to a spiritual paroxysm before they will exert enough effort to effect spiritual change in their lives, but that is a part of our ministry. We are provokers!

The Reason We Provoke

Few leaders enjoy provoking others, and I am unaware of any seminary courses on provoking, but not everyone willingly follows the pastor from one spiritual plane to another. Many Christians are less like submissive sheep and more like stubborn cattle who must be encouraged with an electric prod to move along. Some can be instructed with gentleness as you get their attention, but it often requires severe measures to get that attention. Provoking is an attention-getter.

Among the reasons ministers must be provokers is the fact that the human heart has a propensity for satisfaction with sameness. We would rather be comfortable than challenged, and we prefer the old to the new simply because the old is known. Change makes us feel insecure. Yet our walk in God is called a life, and life must progress or it will regress. The entire New Testament calls for progressive maturation in the lives of believers. This often requires provoking and prodding by spiritual parents. Ministers are commissioned to "provoke unto love and to good works" (Hebrews 10:24, KJV).

Another reason why provoking our brothers and sisters in the Lord is so important is that many of them are imprisoned in their religious traditions. They measure all truth by those traditions, and they examine all spiritual experiences through their doctrinal microscopes. This tends to trap them in sameness and produces an automatic rejection of anything that appears to be new or different. These people need to be forced — provoked — into seeing something different so that they can compare "spiritual things with spiritual" (1 Corinthians 2:13). No one is going to walk out of his entrenched religious traditions unless he has something superior into which to walk. We can often provoke such persons to better things in God by demonstrating these things to them.

Perhaps a major reason ministers must provoke their followers to love and good works is the fact that the natural life dominates most minds to the extent that the spiritual life seems intangible and distant. Paul found it necessary to challenge his converts, "If then you were raised with Christ, seek those things which are above, where Christ is, sitting at the right hand of God. Set your mind on things above, not on things on the earth" (Colossians 3:1, 2). It takes a lot of provoking to keep people's minds on Christ, for most persons change only under great pressure. The world, the flesh, and the devil compete quite successfully for the attention of all of us. Someone needs to provoke our thoughts to God and things spiritual, or we will become carnal Christians with no genuine interest in God.

Even Christians who have a committed relationship with God need to be provoked occasionally lest they too quickly settle for the merely good rather than contend for the best. Every level we attain in Christ is so superior to our former position in God that we think we have finally attained the ultimate, but there are always greater heights to be reached. We need to hear the cry of the prophet " 'Arise and depart, for this is not your rest' " (Micah 2:10). God may allow us to rest on a plateau for a season, but He will not permit us to remain there very long. He will provoke us to resume the climb toward His own presence.

The Persons We Provoke

All of God's ministers are leaders in the Body of Christ. We are commissioned to lead, not to drive, the sheep. We do not point them to the way; we lead them in the way. It is obvious, therefore, that we cannot take the sheep any farther than we have gone, nor will the sheep go any farther than the shepherd leads them. This means that the spiritual level of a church will not rise above the level of its leadership, for the sheep will not be allowed to precede the shepherd.

It is little wonder, then, that Paul exhorted us, "Watch ye, stand fast in the faith, quit you like men, be strong" (1 Corinthians 16:13, KJV). It is true that ministers are watchmen for others, but Paul seemed to be saying to believers, "Watch yourselves!" Ministers need to provoke themselves to "stand fast in the faith, be brave, be strong" (NKJV). If we are not self-motivated in spiritual things, who will motivate us? When Paul wrote to his son in the faith, he told Timothy, "I remind you to stir up the gift of God which is in you through the laying on of my hands" (2 Timothy 1:6). The gift was evident, but it was in danger of becoming dormant through neglect and disuse. Paul wanted Timothy to provoke, or stir, that gift into action.

The root for the Greek word *paroxusmos* means "to sharpen." The context of the Hebrews passage that instructs us to "provoke one another unto love and to good works" lists at least four areas of awareness we need to sharpen before we are qualified to provoke others.

We ministers need to sharpen our awareness of God, for it is possible to be so aware of people and problems that we lose our awareness of God. Hebrews 10:19-21 challenges us to take a fresh look at Jesus, Whose blood gives us the right of access to God (v. 19), Whose flesh has become the route of access (v. 20), and Whose function is that of our High Priest in the presence of God (v. 21). We can provoke our faith to higher levels by looking anew at Jesus. This is imperative in ministers, for "without faith it is impossible to please Him, for he who comes to God must believe that He is, and that He is a rewarder of those who diligently seek Him" (Hebrews 10:22). Ministers need to provoke themselves to a revitalized awareness of companionship with God. We not only have faith in God; we are invited to have fellowship with Him. There is probably no area in a minister's life that meets more opposition than his intimate time with God. Ministers find the discipline of coming to God difficult to maintain. Prayer time is constantly interrupted by "the lust of the flesh, the lust of the eyes, and the pride of life" (1 John 2:16). We must daily provoke ourselves to enjoy time in God's presence.

Ministers are also challenged to "hold fast the confession of our hope [faith, KJV] without wavering" (Hebrews 10:23). Unless we discipline — provoke — ourselves to regularly spend time in God's Word, our hope will diminish, our faith will weaken, and our ministry will perish. We need to review God's promises and reclaim God's provisions, but there are so many things bidding for our time and attention that Bible reading is no longer automatic in the lives of ministers. Many ministers admit to spending little time in the Word. One wonders what sustains their faith and their hope.

A final exhortation encourages us ministers to a vital consideration of the brotherhood. We are told to "consider one another ... not forsaking the assembling of ourselves together" (Hebrews 10:24, 25). Our relationships cannot always be sheep/shepherds; we also need to relate to our brothers and sisters in Christ. Ministers need companionship, too. If we isolate and insulate ourselves from other Christians, we should expect to be attacked by the wolves, for the sheep that straggles behind the flock is the one that becomes prey for the wolves.

Before we are commissioned to provoke others to greater heights in God, we are commanded to provoke — or sharpen — our own lives in God-awareness, companionship-awareness, promise-awareness, and people-awareness, for only the alerted one can sound an alert to others.

Any minister who fails or refuses to provoke himself to godliness runs the risk of indulging slothfulness and is guaranteeing failure in the area of excellence. In addition to this, he is inviting a season of depression, for nothing will go right for him, and his personal and spiritual life will get stale. We need to provoke ourselves to do what we know should be done. It is not what we know that makes us victorious in this life; it is what we do with what we know.

If we ministers will faithfully excite our own lives to "love and good works," we will automatically provoke others to do the same thing, for the power of a personal demonstration is worth a thousand sermons. After sending prophets to Israel for generations, God sent salvation to the Gentiles "to provoke them [the Jews] to jealousy" (Romans 11:11). God's goodness was an irritant and a goad to the Jews, and God's manifest goodness to a leader will always prod some saints to renewed "love and good works." "Show it — don't just say it" is the unspoken cry in the pews of American churches.

This, of course, does not discount the need to say it. We should prod, provoke, and motivate people to righteous living by every form of communication we are capable of using, whether public or private, vocal or written. Every sermon should provoke the listeners to act, not merely to disseminate information, for ministers are responsible to incite people to change, and our speech is a valid tool.

The one person we have not been commissioned to provoke is God; yet we often provoke Him more than we provoke our followers. Speaking of Israel, Moses said, "Then he forsook God who made him, and scornfully esteemed the Rock of his salvation. They provoked Him to jealousy with foreign gods; with abominations they provoked Him to angers' " (Deuteronomy 32:15, 16).

Like God's covenant people in the wilderness, we provoke God with our insistent complaints about the way He is leading us, the provisions with which He is sustaining us, and the persons He has set in office to guide us. There are times when we don't like anything that God does, but that is usually the manifestation of doubt in our hearts.

Other times we provoke God with our disobedience, as Israel did in trying to store manna rather than gather it daily, or with the same rejection of God that caused Israel to plead with Him never to speak to them again in an audible voice. The ten spies were not the last ministers to spread their unbelief through the encampment of God's people, and Israel's rebellion is still contagious. Their acts provoked God to send plagues, punishment, and extreme disabilities upon His people. They still do. May God grant that we will be the right kind of provokers for His sake and ours.

A faithful minister will provoke people; he may provoke God, but he must provoke himself. Stirring others to action is not enough; he must incite himself to action. As Paul told Timothy: "I remind you to stir up the gift of God which is in you ... For God has not given us a spirit of fear, but of power and of love and of a sound mind" (2 Timothy 1:6, 7). The minister must eat what he serves!

Prayer:

O Lord, my very calling makes me a provoker, and the message You have given me to share often seems to be more of an ox-goad than it is good news. Please teach me to provoke myself into your perfect will; by my life may I motivate others to live in perfect communion with You. I long, dear Jesus, to be provoked by You, but I deeply fear provoking You. Please get to me before I can get to You. Amen!

Chapter 18

Leaders as Pray-ers

"I desire that men pray everywhere, lifting up holy hands ..." (1 Timothy 2:7)

Diversity of faith is a major problem among ministers. Actually, most of the divisions in the Body of Christ are caused by these contrasts in concepts. But when the subject of prayer is discussed, there is an immediate commonality among us, for all who are in the Lord's service believe in prayer. Repeatedly, we ministers have been reminded, and, indeed, we have admonished others who were entering into a ministry, "Little prayer, little power; more prayer, more power; much prayer, much power; but no prayer, no power." We have often quoted from Tennyson's *Morte d' Arthur*, "More things are wrought by prayer than this world dreams," and we frequently put the simple motto, "Prayer Changes Things," directly over our desks. At church we sing, "Prayer is the Key to Heaven, but Faith Unlocks the Door," and we lead the congregation in singing, "Sweet Hour of Prayer." It is difficult to find a minister who lacks a consciousness of the value, validity, and vitality of prayer, for every major step we have taken in God was associated with prayer.

Ministers are generally prepared to "offer a word of prayer" at almost a moment's notice and at a great variety of public occasions whether sporting, political, or religious, and the "pastoral prayer" is often viewed as a focal point of the Sunday morning worship service. Whether a minister can preach or not, he is expected to be able to pray both privately and publicly. His congregation depends heavily upon those prayers, often phoning in their needs in the wee hours of the morning.

The Principle of Prayer

Nearly twenty times in the Gospels, Jesus commanded His disciples to pray, and Paul quite consistently pled with the churches to pray for him. The New Testament exhibits great praying, exhorts us to fervent praying, and explains prayer to us. Prayer is never presented as optional for the Christian believer; it is always declared to be obligatory, for we can't function effectively without it. Perhaps this is why all Christian leaders believe in the principle of prayer.

In our early studies of Church history, we were overwhelmed with the stories of the lives of great praying men such as George Muller in England, Praying Hyde in India and Robert Brainert among the American Indians. We mentally classified them among the spiritual giants alongside Moses, Elijah, and Isaiah, and we marvelled at what was accomplished through their prayers. Their lives beautifully underscored the principle of prayer for us.

From our pulpits and in our fellowship groups we point to Daniel's powerful praying, and how Elijah closed, and then later opened, the heavens with his fervent prayers. We preach series of sermons on the prayers of Paul, and we regularly lead our congregations in the recitation of the Lord's Prayer. We firmly believe in prayer — especially someone else's prayers.

The Parrying of Prayer

Perhaps many ministers are like Christ's disciples who willingly rowed the boat across the Sea of Galilee while Jesus spent the night in prayer. These disciples, you realize, were not men of prayer, they were men of action. They were far too busy organizing the crowds, securing the food supply for the entourage, and protecting Jesus from people to give themselves to prayer. They were need-centered, not God-conscious. Repeatedly, they proved themselves to be earthly minded rather than spiritually minded, and they were obviously kingdom-oriented more than they were in love with the king.

Perhaps we should not be too critical of them, for they were raised in the religious system of the day, which emphasized behavior rather than relationship. Furthermore, they had at least four reasons for parrying their responsibility to pray: self-reliance, self-centeredness, success, and a suitable substitute.

These ministers of Christ's choosing were men of *self-reliance*. When Jesus commanded them to feed the multitude, they quickly reported to Jesus that their combined assets wouldn't even purchase enough bread for each person to get a taste, and when Jesus told them that they would flee from Him and even betray Him, Peter loudly proclaimed that he would never do such a thing, no matter what the other disciples might do. Since Peter had such trust in himself, what need did he have for prayer?

The disciples were also very *self-centered*. Their dispute over how they were to be seated in the kingdom displays this. There seems to have been so much

infighting over who would be the greatest in the
kingdom that Jesus girded Himself with a towel and
washed the feet of the disciples to demonstrate to them
that greatness was measured in service rather than in
position. Since it is impossible to be both self-centered
and God-centered, it is to be expected that these men
would be prayerless in their daily lives.

Still a third reason for prayerlessness among the
disciples was their great *success* in their ministry.
Hadn't the loaves and fishes multiplied in their very
hands while they served them to the multitude? They
had cast out devils, healed the sick, cleansed the lepers,
and preached the Gospel of the kingdom. Israel had not
seen such demonstration of Divine power for hundreds
of years. What need had they for prayer when they
were possessors of such power?

Furthermore, these disciples didn't feel that they
needed to pray, for they had a *suitable substitute* in
their midst in the person of Jesus, Who was a great man
of prayer. He had such great contact with the Father
that they could comfortably leave all spiritual responsibilities to Him. They had observed that whatever
Jesus asked of the Father was immediately granted.
Likely, the disciples mentally put prayer in Christ's
department and placed performance in theirs. It was
an early concept of team ministry.

The way they parried prayer has come down
through the centuries as a legacy to subsequent disciples. Although ministers hear about prayer, talk about
prayer, preach on prayer, and even schedule prayer
meetings, few ministers actually give themselves to
prayer. Early in 1986, the Gallup poll was commissioned
to do a survey of professional ministers in America.
Among the questions asked in this survey was, "How
much time do you spend in daily prayer?" The national
average was ten (10) minutes. Just 10 out of 1440
minutes in the day! Why is so little time budgeted for

prayer? Perhaps the same four "S's" that the disciples used to parry prayer are used today.

Today's ministers are given to *self-reliance*. They have their college degrees, their denominational backing, and their committees. Their financial security is in their paychecks, parsonages, and pensions. They get their guidance from boards, committees, and elders, and their programs have likely been established by their predecessors, while their sermons come from books and tapes. What need have they for prayer? They have all the bases covered.

Unfortunately, the modern minister is apt to be as *self-centered* as the disciples were. Most denominations have infighting and politicking for position and honor that would make the disciples look like amateurs. Many pastors seek more to be served by their people than to become servants to those persons, and the key word in their conversations is *my* — *my* church, *my* program and *my* ministry. If they were to pray an honest prayer it would be, "Nevertheless, not Thy will, but *mine* be done." Since their lives and ministries revolve around themselves, it is nearly impossible for them to pray, for prayer demands a mind that is centered upon God.

To the surprise of many of us, these ministers sometimes achieve a great measure of success. They build congregations and buildings; get promoted to honorific positions; establish nationwide radio and television ministries, and are often seen as men and women of great faith and power. What is overlooked is that these ministers, like the disciples of Christ, are functioning on conferred authority, which is limited in nature, location, and time. The disciples were ecstatic at their abilities to cast out demons on their commissioned trip into the towns and villages around Jerusalem, but they were utterly powerless to cleanse the demonized boy while Christ was on the mount of transfiguration. When they asked Jesus why they had failed they were told, "This kind does not go out except by prayer and fasting" (Matthew 17:21). This problem did not come under the prior authority that had been conferred to them. They were not in the area to which they had been sent, the timing of that sending was over, and the demonic force at work was a higher force than they had been commissioned to deal with. Perhaps the conferred authority of the gifts of the Spirit have limitations that the authority of relationship with God does not have. In any case, when power is used as an excuse from prayer it generally runs its course and is exhausted, leaving only ritual of behavior and memories of past successes.

How do such persons survive in the ministry? They seek *suitable substitutes* to pray for them, just as the disciples did. Oh, how pastors like to brag about their "intercessors" who touch the heavens on behalf of the church. This select, and often small, group of praying persons, predominantly women, take needs to God and bring answers back from God to the pastor. Thank God for these praying persons who have actually kept Divine life and light in situations that would have become dead and dark, but is an intercessors' group a proper substitute for ministerial prayer, or should it be a powerful supplement? I have seen pastors take direction from intercessors that led the local church into tremendous confusion, for that word was not a confirmation of something God had spoken in his heart, it was outside direction from a fallible being whose self-interests may well have influenced what he or she communicated to the pastor.

The Practice of Prayer

As long as the disciples had a substitute, they did not pray. They talked about praying, they felt guilty for not praying, and they even asked for a lesson on prayer, but they worked or slept while Jesus did the praying. Then Jesus left them, and religion turned against them. They were jailed, stoned, driven from their homes, and persecuted beyond measure. Their status was gone, their security was stripped from them, and there was no one to do their praying for them. They had asked the Lord to teach them *to* pray (not how to pray), and He had turned their smug little self-centered world upside-down until it was pray or perish. Isn't it amazing what can be done when it is a do-or-die situation?

For those ministers who would rather parry prayer than participate in prayer, God has a tailor-made set of circumstances to bring them to their knees, and when they do get involved in prayer, they discover that prayer is far more than functional, it is relational. As long as we view prayer as merely functional, we will pray in crises, but we will abandon prayer in times of calm. While "prayer changes things," its most valuable service is that it changes us. Prayer changes our concepts of God and our ideas about communicating with Him. We cease viewing prayer as time-consuming and see it as time-saving, and we stop seeing prayer as being about the work of the church and discover that prayer *is* the work of the Church. We abandon using Christ as a means to an end, and we begin to accept Christ as the true end of prayer. Prayer ceases being a way to get something from God, and it becomes a way to get to God. None of this can be learned from a book — not even this book. It is learned only in personal prayer.

Today's generation of milk-fed Christians tend to see prayer as a means of giving God "unknown" information, a channel for expressing our "want-list," and a vehicle by which we give commands to God. This keeps prayer on a very low level where everything is basically centered upon ourselves. There is, of course, a place for petition in prayer, but "give me" is barely above the lowest prayer of "forgive me."

God would like to have His spiritual leaders mature in praying until prayer can be seen and used as communion with God, conversation with God, or meditation on God. If any of today's ministers are going to be called "The Friend of God" (James 2:23), they must learn to fellowship with God and delight in His presence, for friends are more than informers and petitioners — they are communicators and companions.

One of the most common complaints from those in full-time ministry is loneliness. Because they are consistently responded to as the leader, the authority, and the expert, they stand alone and aloof. Often their attempts to reach out to other ministers are rebuffed by the tremendous spirit of competition that exists between American churches, so the minister becomes a loner. Prayer is the first and most important step in moving out of isolation. It releases a person from aloneness, and it brings the praying person into such fellowship with God that he or she soon discovers that in prayer no one is ever alone.

What will it take to bring American ministers back into a praying relationship with God? Severe persecution, utter failure, or moral breakdown often forces ministers to their knees, but these are drastic measures. Wouldn't it be far simpler to effect an attitude change? We who are in the service of the Lord of Hosts need to understand that prayer is more than what it does. If God never said yes to any petition we presented, the time spent in praying would not have been wasted, for we are praying, not because of crises, but because of Christ. The value of prayer is far more the effects of prayer upon us than the receiving of the things for which we petitioned. Prayer will become communication between love partners.

The story is told of a small girl who told her mother she was going to her bedroom to pray to Jesus. When for a protracted season the tot failed to come out of her room, the mother stuck her head in the doorway to the bedroom to ask what she was doing.

"I was just telling Jesus that I love Him and He was telling me that He loves me. And we were just loving each other," she innocently replied.

Is there a better example of true prayer?

Isn't it about time we ministers got off our thrones and onto our knees? The present failure rate should convince us that God's way cannot fail, but our substitutes will always fail. We need to stop merely preaching about prayer and begin praying. We must eat what we serve!

Prayer:

Dear Jesus, forgive me for my prayerlessness. I know I am called to Your service, and I am completely willing to serve, but I have discovered that I am not capable of spiritual ministry. Please teach me the dependence upon the Father that You exhibited while You were here on this earth. Please help me not to exchange activity for relationship, and may I not accept old commissions for present ministry. Help me to hear Your voice regularly, get my instructions daily, and enjoy Your presence hourly, for without You I am nothing and I can do nothing of spiritual value. Amen!

Chapter 19

Leaders as Pupils

"Give attention to reading" (1 Timothy 4:13)

For those ministers who disciplined themselves to formal training, graduation day was an exciting event, whether they received merely a Bible school certificate or an earned doctoral degree. It signified the culmination of years of study, and it was public recognition of achievement. The document presented was quickly framed and hung on the wall in the study or office, and with a sense of deep satisfaction, the graduate read the formal words on the credential, sighed an exclamation of relief, and said, "Now I am a minister!"

The only anxiety that now remained was for an assignment to a parish where the years of learning could be put into use and imparted to the hungry faithful we would serve. We were ready to take on the world with all of its problems. Faculty, studies, and books were behind us now; we would be the teachers from now on. How fortunate this church would be to have as its pastor one who knows so much!

It didn't take long for most of us to realize that the academic studies in which we had invested years of our lives were quite useless in meeting the needs of people. Somehow, notes from the class sessions that had been so very exciting to us seemed boring to our parishioners. They couldn't even understand the necessity of knowing the Hebrew and Greek languages, and their grasp of theology was so limited they couldn't comfortably follow our vocabularies.

Most of us who have been in the service of the Lord for many years now wish that we knew half as much as we thought we knew when we graduated. We have since discovered that our college education was less an acquisition of knowledge and more an introduction to where knowledge could be found. We have slowly learned to distill academic knowledge into practical truth, and now accept that we do not have all the answers.

The frustration of ministry has sent many ministers back to the classrooms to earn higher and higher degrees, while other pastors step from the pulpit into the business world with a very real sense of failure gnawing at them emotionally. In spite of their schooling, they felt that they did not know enough to continue in the ministry.

They were right, you know. None of us knows enough to be capable ministers of the Divine grace of our Lord Jesus Christ, but we know more than we used to know, and we are perpetual students through life. At whatever point a minister renounces being a pupil, he condemns himself to sameness and dullness.

Even the learned Apostle Paul testified, "Brethren, I do not count myself to have apprehended; but one thing I do, forgetting those things which are behind and reaching forward to those things which are ahead, I press toward the goal for the prize of the upward call of God in Christ Jesus" (Philippians 3:13-14).

Pupils in the School of the Spirit

Jesus knew the need for a continuing education in the experience of His disciples, so He promised to send His Spirit to dwell in them, and said, "when He, the Spirit of truth, has come, He will guide you into all truth; for He will not speak on His own authority, but whatever He hears He will speak; and He will tell you things to come. He will glorify Me, for He will take of what is Mine and declare it to you" (John 16:13, 14). Whereas we once went to the teacher, now the Teacher comes to us.

What a Teacher the Holy Spirit is! He can make God's Word come alive like the burning bush in the wilderness of Sinai. He can illuminate truth that even a knowledge of the original languages cannot unravel. He can link together passages from the Old and New Testaments that reveal God to us in new dimensions, very much as Jesus did after His resurrection while walking with the disciples on the road to Emaus.

Even when we are miles away from our offices, the Holy Spirit continues to instruct us by an inner voice. Jesus said, " 'the Holy Spirit, whom the Father will send in My name, He will teach you all things, and bring to your remembrance all things that I said to you' " (John 14:26). Not all truth unfolds as the result of conscious study. Some of the most glorious truths that I have learned have come to me while my mind was relaxed enough to hear the inner voice of the Spirit speaking to me. At first I thought that my mind was involved in imagination, but when I found that what I had "imagined" was actually in the Bible, I learned to listen to the Spirit within me. He teaches so gently, but what we learn from Him becomes life-changing.

Other times, the Spirit teaches us through the lips of others. More times than we might want to admit, a "chance" remark of another turns on a light of illumination in our minds that unveils a whole new avenue of truth. The speaker is not always a theologian, for God communicates His truth to us through the learned and the unlearned; through men and women, and through the converted and the unconverted. If God could speak to the prophet Balaam through the mouth of a donkey, He certainly can speak to us through any channel that is available to Him. The key is not the speaking mouth, but the listening ear.

We need to know the voice of the Spirit no matter how it is communicated. When speaking in the metaphor of a shepherd, Jesus said, "the sheep follow him, for they know his voice" (John 10:4). This is acquired, not inherent, knowledge. Sheep are not born knowing the voice of the shepherd; they learn to distinguish his voice from the voices of other persons through their relationship with the shepherd and with other sheep who have acquired that knowledge. We learn to distinguish the voice of the Spirit in the same way. It, too, is a learned ability. We acquire a listening ear through diligent comparison and daily relationship. Fortunately, God has given us His Word as a touchstone of the Spirit's inner communication, for God will never speak contrary to His written Word. What safety this is for us pupils.

We will never graduate from the school of the Spirit; we are merely promoted to higher levels of learning. But, then, who would want to graduate from such a glorious school? It is likely that throughout all of eternity the same Spirit will be unfolding mystery after mystery about God and His Kingdom.

Pupils in the School of Life

Ministers are not only pupils in the Spirit's school; they are always enrolled in the school of life. None of us is an island, nor does anyone have all the pieces of the puzzle. We must learn and receive from one another or be forever confined in the narrow canyon of our discovery.

Jesus taught, " 'Therefore every scribe instructed concerning the kingdom of heaven is like a householder who brings out of his treasure things new and old' " (Matthew 13:52). The "old treasures" are principles we have lived and tested plus truths that we have fully digested, while the "new treasures" are likely fresh revelations and concepts recently acquired. Only a pupil can bring forth new treasure, but a parrot can express new words.

Some of this new treasure comes from our enrollment in the school of the Spirit, but much of it comes from being observant pupils in the school of life. What has been well known to others is often fresh and new to us when we see it. That's why it is so important to expose ourselves to what others are seeing — even if we disagree with it initially.

No generation has had such an availability of different concepts as today's American Christians. We have Christian television, radio, cassettes, and a proliferation of Christian books. While this can be confusing, it can also be educational. Paul told Timothy, "Give attention to reading" (1 Timothy 4:13), and his message is still applicable to today's generation of ministers. We need to know what God shared with the early reformers, the Puritans, the pioneer pentecostals, and others, and we also need to hear what God is saying to different persons in our own generation.

In much of the business community, success or failure depends upon keeping current, and this requires a vast amount of reading. No one wants to submit himself to a doctor who knows medicine only as it was taught in the early twenties, nor would we call a computer repairman who knows only the old tube circuits of the World War II-vintage computers. We want persons who are current in their fields; so do our congregations.

Knowledge is progressive — even spiritual knowledge. We need to "grow in the grace and knowledge of our Lord and Savior Jesus Christ" (2 Peter 3:18). Paul prayed "that your love may abound still more and more in knowledge and all discernment" (Philippians 1:9), and "that you may be filled with the knowledge of His will in all wisdom and spiritual understanding ... increasing in the knowledge of God" (Colossians 1:9, 10). And it was this same Paul who ask Timothy to "bring ... the books, especially the parchments" (2 Timothy 4:13). This great minister of divine revelation was obviously also a man of much reading. He valued what had already been said alongside of what was being newly said.

The minister who will not discipline himself to regularly read imprisons himself in sameness. He will continue to repeat the same tired concepts, using worn-out religious phrases and cliches until they lose all meaning both to himself and to his hearers.

Obviously, books are not the only teaching medium in the school of life; experience is a keen instructor. Living has always been an education in its own right. We ministers must learn beyond our own personal experiences. We need to learn about life as other people view, experience, and respond to it. Few ministers consistently preach to theologians; we share truth with people who do not live in our isolated ivory towers, and we need to know what they are facing in the workaday world. We need to get out of the study into the workplace from time to time, and we must cultivate the ability to genuinely listen to people when they talk to us. We will better meet their needs if we truly understand their problems, and in those times when we are unable to meet their needs we can at least offer our understanding presence.

Pupils in the School of Hard Knocks

Graduation from seminary does not mean that we have graduated from the school of hard knocks, nor is ordination insulation from hardship. Christian service is involvement in a conflict, not isolation from contention. The minister not only wades through his own rough places in life; he shares in the conflicts and confusions of the members of his congregation. Furthermore, he often becomes the target of the enemy whenever the congregation enters into spiritual victories.

Having said, "Since we have this ministry," Paul admitted "we are hard pressed on every side, yet not crushed; we are perplexed, but not in despair; persecuted, but not forsaken; struck down, but not destroyed" (2 Corinthians 4:1, 8, 9). The Knox, Williams, and Phillips translations of the New Testament handle that final phrase as: "We are knocked down, but not knocked out." We may be bruised, but we are not buried.

Hardships, reverses, opposition, misunderstandings, and even some failures are to be expected — they are par for the course. The successful minister is the one who has learned from these hard knocks, not the one who has managed to avert all negatives. We must let all of these disagreeable experiences be our instructors. Few of us learn much in pleasant experiences, but all of us should learn much from the unpleasant ones. Perhaps Belheimer's book *Don't Waste Your Sorrows* should be must reading for every minister.

All of us who are in the ministry should be good students of our own selves. We need to know our personal signals of fatigue and heed them. God will never wear a person out, but religion regularly does so. Overextension is a common sin for ministers, and it forces them to work in the midst of high fatigue, eventually leading to burnout. The person who has been a good pupil to his body will learn to pronounce the word *no* with great authority.

Equally, we ministers also need to come to grips with our emotions so we can recognize the early indications of depression and anxiety. Knowing our emotions enables us to either be guided by them or to rule over them, but when we confuse honest emotional signals as spiritual messages we will not only live confused lives; we will share a confused ministry.

Furthermore, we need to understand our motivations. A good student of himself begins to understand some of the "whys" that rule his or her behavior. When we know what drives us, we can harness and utilize this in the work of the Lord. Good self-starters in the ministry are persons who know what gets them going and have learned to use it.

Admittedly, not all ministers remain as pupils for their whole life. Some become so engaged in "doing" that they cease caring about "being." These persons usually seek early retirement, or they complain loudly about burnout.

If we get so locked into what we've learned that we refuse to learn anything further, we will, obviously, become very dated, and soon will be seriously outdated. We'll contend earnestly [contentiously?] for old truths with a mind so closed it cannot receive any new concepts, and we may very well find ourselves opposing any who claim to see something that we do not see. It is almost axiomatic that the persecuted of one generation become the persecutors of the next. It has been pointed out that fresh moves of God come through new leadership, and both Bible and Church history tend to show that the leadership of the old had to be buried before the new leadership could come on the scene. Is this God's caprice or is it our limited capacity? Didn't Joshua and Caleb join the young army in the conquest of Canaan? They seemed to keep their vision current and their faith active. They didn't talk about Egypt, nor did they seem to spend much time talking about "the good old days" of the wilderness. They had caught a glimpse of the future, and they were determined to become a part of it.

We ministers need to get back in school and remain there. We constantly tell our congregations to "study to shew thyself approved unto God" (2 Timothy 2:15, KJV). Isn't it about time that we practice what we preach? As pupils we need to eat what we serve!

Prayer:

Dear Lord, forgive me for relying so heavily upon what I have learned, and help me be a consistent student. Teach me to open my eyes to spiritual truths everywhere I go. Help me to hear the voice of the Spirit in the quiet hours of the night, and in the busy hours of the day. Let me learn from the experiences I am continually sharing in life, and keep me fresh that I may be a participant with You in every new thing You purpose to do during my lifetime. Refire me; don't retire me. Renew me; don't refuse me. Give me a word that is as fresh to the coming generation as it was to my grandparents. Don't let me get dated in the things of the Spirit. Amen!

Chapter 20

Leaders as Pursuers

" 'Will You pursue dry stubble?' " (Job 13:25)

It is not without significance that when Paul was talking about his ministry he said, "Do you not know that those who run in a race all run, but one receives the prize? Run in such a way that you may obtain it. And everyone who competes for the prize is temperate in all things. Now they do it to obtain a perishable crown, but we for an imperishable crown" (1 Corinthians 9:24, 25). Running is an appropriate illustration of a minister's lifestyle, for the calling and commission of the ministry demand strong drive and determination. Quite often the competitive drive of an athlete becomes a useful force in the life of one who has dedicated himself or herself to a life of ministering to others.

A minister lives in a constant chase. His motto could well be, "The hurrieder I go, the behinder I get." Ministry is a perpetual following in order to overtake, much as a coyote pursues a rabbit. A successful catch only means seeking another rabbit to chase.

The word *pursue* occurs quite frequently as a command in the Old Testament. It is a translation of the Hebrew word *radaph*, which signifies "to run after, chase, follow after, hunt, or put to flight." Pastors, especially, run after the strays, chase the lambs, follow after the flock, hunt fresh pastures, and put to flight the predators, but pursuing is not limited exclusively to pastors, for all ministers are involved in a perpetual pursuit. It is part of our calling.

The Pursuit of Good

Probably all conscientious ministers begin with a pursuit of good, for the command of the Word is, "Always pursue what is good both for yourselves and for all" (1 Thessalonians 5:15). It is this very quest that opened their hearts to the call of God in the first place. Like Adam in the garden of Eden, they sought to know what was good by learning to commune with a good God; the more they came to know God, the stronger was their desire to pursue good, until it became a powerful motivational drive in their lives. So obvious is this to the world that persons who dedicate themselves to ministry are often dubbed "do-gooders." Having pursued good, they became proclaimers of good to anyone who would listen to them, for, after all, the Gospel is "good news."

When Paul was exhorting his son in the faith to beware of lusting after money and earthly possessions, he gave a very positive position for Timothy to take: "But you, O man of God, flee these things and pursue righteousness, godliness, faith, love, patience, gentleness" (1 Timothy 6:11). Paul was convinced that successful ministry is more than abandoning worldly goals; it is the pursuit of heavenly goals. Greed and the love of money are to be replaced with a passion for righteousness and godliness. The wise man said, "He who follows righteousness and mercy finds life, righteousness and honor" (Proverbs 21:21) and "He [the Lord] loves him who follows righteousness" (Proverbs 15:9).

The pursuit of godliness is a combination of pursuing love, holiness, and peace, for God is defined as "love," "holy," and "peace" (see 1 John 4:16; Revelation 4:8; Isaiah 9:6). The Bible commands us in no uncertain terms to pursue these three components of godliness, for it is written, "Pursue love" (1 Corinthians 14:1) and "Pursue peace with all men, and holiness ..." (Hebrews 12:14). A quick glance at a concordance will reveal that other passages in Scripture equally challenge us to pursue these graces with a fervency.

Of course, these are not the only good things a person in the ministry is challenged to pursue. Paul told Timothy to also pursue "faith ... patience, [and] gentleness" (1 Timothy 6:11), and the saints in Rome were exhorted, "therefore let us pursue the things which make for peace and the things by which one may edify another" (Romans 14:19). We ministers should pursue these things with the same care, attention, and diligence that wild animals demonstrate in hunting their prey. It dare not be only an occasional function, for our lives depend upon both pursuing and capturing these graces.

The Pursuit of Goals

Somewhere in the life of a minister, especially one who is in the full-time or professional ministry, his pursuit shifts from good to goals, partially because we live in a goal-oriented society. Frequently, these goals are the three "S's" and the three "P's" that dominate both our secular and religious society today: success, size, and security; position, power, and possessions.

Very early in his career a minister gets bitten by the *success* bug. His attendance at religious conferences and his reading of Christian publications endue him with an ambition to "succeed," whatever that word may mean to him at the time. Forgetting that he is but a servant of the Lord, he begins to plan strategy that will enable him to be successful. This may include a building program, whether he actually needs new facilities or not, or a return to college to upgrade his educational degree.

No minister dares set his sights to fail, but when he sets his heart on success he had better have a clear understanding of what God calls success, for throughout the Scriptures men who have achieved God's blessing and approval have not always met the standards that our generation sets for "success." Some prophets were totally rejected, and many of them were martyred for their message. Inspired writers had their books burned by the king himself, and thousands of priests ministered selflessly for their entire lives without even having their names recorded in sacred history. Still, these persons were approved by God, even in the midst of their rejection by men, because they were faithfully obedient to a Divine task.

Success is a fickle thing to pursue, but so is a passion for *size*. This is the religious generation of the mega-church. Throughout the world we are witnessing the development of local congregations that number into multiple thousands of people. Church-growth conventions are regularly convened, and methods and motivational lectures are given to pastors, who often begin to pursue the second "S": *size*. Growth for the Kingdom's sake is great, but growth for growth's sake can be a snare that prevents a minister from doing the task God gave to him. Large is not sacred to God, nor is small holy. Obedience and faithfulness are God's goals for His ministers, not lust for numbers or copying the actions of another who gained those numbers. The early Christian Church grew to mega-size not through entertainment, drives, programs, or the ambitions of the Apostles, nor as the result of conscious desire;

growth was a byproduct of continual teaching, fellow-shipping and prayers (*see* Acts 2:42). "The Lord added to the church daily those who were being saved" (Acts 2:47).

If success and size are achieved, the third "S" that ministers tend to pursue is *security*. It is usually assumed that a "successful" minister who has established a sizable work should be assured financial independence and security. Somehow, the simple, childlike trust in God that got them where they are is set aside for the security that their Kingdom can provide for them. They forget that God made Israel gather manna daily, except on the Sabbath, to keep a perpetual faith operative.

If security is reached, can the pursuit of *position* be very far away? The American philosophy that hard work brings promotion can so infiltrate our minds as to cause the most honorable among us to expect to move up the religious ladder just because we are industrious and somewhat successful. Staff members strive for the title of "assistant pastor," and pastors begin calling themselves "apostles." The more ambitious among them begin political jockeying for a denominational office. I have known men with quality pulpit ministries to surrender them for a desk job as an accountant for their denominational headquarters because it carried the title of "District Treasurer." Position was more important to them than ministry, and often that office cost them all spiritual ministry. It was a successful pursuit, but the price was trading a Divine calling for an organizational position.

My father-in-law maintained a dairy herd during World War II, and he often said that the only two cows in his herd that were completely contented were the lead cow and the last cow in line. All the rest were constantly pushing and shoving for a better position in the line. How often this same principle is seen among the ministers of the Gospel. Being "number one" seems important enough to jostle, jab, and jockey for that position. It's like the impatient driver who passes us, weaving dangerously from lane to lane, but we meet him again at the stoplight down the road. He may have gained a car length, but he risked his life in doing so.

It seems inherent in most persons to want to dominate another, and this trait is especially strong in leaders, whether that leadership is in the financial, political, or spiritual realm. The pursuit of power is a tangent onto which satan often succeeds in detouring ministers. God offers spiritual power to those who maintain a close relationship with Him, but oftentimes ecclesiastical, psychological, or positional power is substituted for the power of God's Spirit. This may indeed give the minister control over others, but it will not become an enablement for ministry, for God declared through the prophet, "Not by might nor by power, but by my Spirit,'' says the LORD of hosts' " (Zechariah 4:6). Spiritual ministry can be exercised only in the power of God's Spirit. Paul chidingly asked the saints, "Are you so foolish? Having begun in the Spirit, are you now being made perfect by the flesh?" (Galatians 3:3). All forms of fleshly power are self-serving and short-lived and will always fall short of meeting spiritual needs. It is a wasted pursuit, for even if it is successful, the rewards slip through the fingers like dry sand.

The third "P" that ministers often pursue, especially in the later years of their ministry, is *possessions.* Failing to understand how empty this pursuit has proved for the unconverted, many ministers fall into this same lust for things, and shopping for, collecting, and driving "the best" become passions in their lives. Perhaps some of this desire is occasioned by a subconscious awareness that life is fast slipping away, and they feel that their sacrifice for ministry has cheated them out of living. In their failure to realize that they are but representatives of a heavenly King and that their rewards are awaiting them in God's Kingdom, they strive to amass the maximum possible number of toys before they die. Someone has said that the person who has the most toys at the time of his death wins, but Paul testified, "I have fought the good fight, I have finished the race, I have kept the faith. Finally, there is laid up for me the crown or righteousness, which the Lord, the righteous Judge, will give to me on that Day, and not to me only but also to all who have loved His appearing" (2 Timothy 4:7, 8).

Possessions should never be the object of our pursuit; they should be a byproduct of our relationship with God. Jesus said, " 'Seek first the kingdom of God and His righteousness, and all these things shall be added to you' " (Matthew 6:33). God would like "things" to be something that He adds as a bonus, not something we pursue with a passion.

The Pursuit of God

At least eighteen times, the Gospels credit Christ with saying, "Follow Me." The primary pursuit for all ministers should be the pursuit of God Himself. This is our calling, and everything that God does to us and through us is fundamentally to assist us in the pursuit, for God is not interested in our service so much as in ourselves.

God, not good, is the ultimate entity we should pursue. When Paul wrote from prison telling of his heritage, zeal, and righteousness, he summarized by saying, "But indeed I also count all things loss for the excellence of the knowledge of Christ Jesus my Lord, for whom I have suffered the loss of all things, and count them as rubbish, *that I may gain Christ*" (Philippians 3:8, emphasis added). Good is great, and often it is the beginning pursuit of one called into the ministry, but God is better. Good is not God, but God is a good God. When we capture a measure of God we automatically gain a great measure of true goodness, but the goodness is now a byproduct of God. The prophet had the priorities correct when he wrote, "It is time to seek the LORD, till He comes and rains righteousness on you" (Hosea 10:12).

If good is a weak object for our pursuit, goals must be totally worthless for that quest. The apostle Paul summarized his pursuit desires in saying, "That I may know Him and the power of His resurrection" and, admitting that he had not yet arrived, added, "I press toward the goal for the prize of the *upward call of God in Christ Jesus.* Therefore let us, as many as are mature, have this mind" (Philippians 3:10, 14, 15, emphasis added).

It is this upward call that should be the object of every mature minister's pursuit. We certainly should not set our hearts on things of this earth when we have been challenged, called, and qualified to seek the Creator of this earth and of everything in it. Of what value are success, size, security, positions, power, or possessions if in achieving them we lost Christ? The Word challenges us, "If then you were raised with Christ, seek those things which are above, where Christ is, sitting at the right hand of God. Set your mind on things above, not on things on the earth. For you died, and your life is hidden with Christ in God" (Colossians 3:1-3). Our Divine life and our heavenly citizenship should keep our desires, and our drives to achieve those desires, focused on spiritual rather than natural things. The psalmists knew this, for they wrote, "The young lions lack and suffer hunger; but those who seek the LORD shall not lack any good thing" (Psalm 34:10). As we seek God, He seeks our good! As we give ourselves to God, He delights in giving Himself to us.

As we set our affections upon Him, He releases His love to us, and He can both outgive and outlove us at any point. David's testimony was "You, LORD, have not forsaken those who seek You" (Psalm 9:10).

When king Saul was pursuing David and entered David's secret hiding place, David refused to kill the king. He merely cut off a corner of the royal robe. Later he called to Saul, showing this evidence of mercy. David cried, " 'After whom has the king of Israel come out? Whom do you pursue? A dead dog? A flea?' " (1 Samuel 24:14). One wonders if many of today's ministers have not joined Saul in mustering an army of 3,000 soldiers to pursue an object as worthless as a dead dog or a flea. The inflamed passions of the moment make the pursuit seem expedient, but all of the energy, effort and expense have been poured out on a worthless project. It would be far better if they would "seek the LORD and His strength; seek His face evermore" (Psalm 105:4).

We have not been called to pursue life or ministry; we have been called to pursue God. He is our life, and He becomes the strength of our life. Everything we will ever need in the course of our ministry can be found in Him, for He is our wisdom, our power and our source of supply. Wisely did the prophet cry, "Seek the LORD while He may be found, call upon Him while He is near" (Isaiah 55:6), for if we pursue the byproducts of ministry rather than God Himself, we may find ourselves out of calling range. David declared, "When You said, 'Seek My face,' my heart said to You, 'Your face, LORD, I will seek' " (Psalm 27:8). We must pursue the Lord with such timing and tenacity as to find Him, and in finding Him, we will discover a whole new source of ministry — a ministry unto God. Since what we pursue determines what the people will pursue, it is imperative that we pursue the highest goal: Christ Jesus Himself. In so doing we will eat what we serve!

Prayer:

Lord, forgive me for pursuing the vain, empty things that consume the hearts of the unconverted, and cause me to seek You with my whole heart. You called me into Your ministry, but I have become so occupied with people, needs, and my own desires that I have forgotten that Your call was unto Yourself, not to do things on Your behalf. Once again stir the cords of my heart until the melody of heaven produces a love song in my soul. I choose, this very day, to redirect my life into a pursuit of the One Who has loved me and called me unto Himself. Amen!

Destiny Image

Read these other dynamic books

from Destiny Image,
The Prophetic Publisher!

Prophets and Personal Prophecy
by Dr. Bill Hamon

The Inner Dimension
by Mark Chironna

His Manifest Presence
by Don Nori

The Church Triumphant
by Nate Krupp

Send for free full-color catalog for a complete list and descriptions of all available titles.

Available through your local Christian bookstore or by writing:

Destiny Image
P.O. Box 351
Shippensburg, PA 17257
Phone orders 1-717-532-3040